The Walls of Windy Troy

The Walls of Windy Troy

A BIOGRAPHY OF HEINRICH SCHLIEMANN

Marjorie Braymer

Illustrated with two diagrams
and one map

A VOYAGER BOOK
HARCOURT, BRACE & WORLD, INC.
New York

Library of Congress Catalog Card Number: 60-6207

Printed in the United States of America

For my students
and
for George and Marianna Packard,
good friends

οὔ τοι ἔπειθ᾽ ἁλίη ὁδὸς ἔσσεται οὐδ᾽ ἀτέλεστος.
—*Odyssey*, II, 273

ACKNOWLEDGMENTS

The author owes thanks to many people who have given assistance in the preparation of this book. Particular and grateful acknowledgment is due the following authors, publishers, agencies, and individuals:

The University of Cincinnati and Princeton University Press, for permission to reproduce charts from *Troy*, Volumes I and III, by Blegen, Caskey, Rawson, and Sperling, copyright 1950, 1953, by Princeton University Press.

Harvard University Press for permission to use brief quotations from *Schliemann's First Visit to America*, edited by Shirley H. Weber and copyright 1942 by the President and Fellows of Harvard College.

Franz J. Horch Associates, Mrs. Emil Ludwig, and Little, Brown and Company for permission to use brief quotations from *Schliemann, The Story of a Gold-Seeker*, by Emil Ludwig, copyright 1931 by Little, Brown and Company.

Scott, Foresman and Company for permission to adapt the time chart from *Civilization Past and Present*, Vol. I, by Wallbank and Taylor, copyright 1942 by Scott, Foresman and Company, Chicago.

Marguerite Yourcenar, Doubleday and Company, and Mr. Melvin Lasky for permission to use a quotation from *Notebooks on Memoirs of Hadrian*, by Marguerite Your-

cenar, from *The Anchor Review*, Doubleday Anchor
Books, copyright 1957 by Doubleday and Company.

Anne Burns, librarian of Sequoia High School, Redwood
City, has been generously helpful with details of research,
and Jeanne Maurer Shutes has my gratitude for her translations from the *Iliad* and the *Odyssey*.

". . . Never lose sight of the graph of a human life, which is not composed, whatever people may say, of a horizontal and two perpendiculars, but rather of three curving lines, drawn out to infinity, forever meeting and forever diverging: what a man has believed himself to be, what he wished to be, and what he was."

—MARGUERITE YOURCENAR

FOREWORD

Anyone familiar with the outlines of Heinrich Schliemann's life may find that in one or two places this narrative disagrees with or may contradict other published biographical materials. When Schliemann wrote of his early years, he was summoning up old memories, and many of them had been overshadowed by the dramatic occurrences of his later life. He was inclined, very understandably, I think, to look back with nostalgia. I found several minor errors in his accounts of early events. For example, it is Shirley H. Weber, editor of the journal of Schliemann's first American trip, who points out that while he did become a United States citizen, this was not in 1850, as his own records have it, but in 1869. The tendency to *will* events into shapes and patterns that would accord best with his desires was a life-long characteristic of the man. To it might be attributed many of his successes as well as his mistakes. In my view, this aspect of his character was, paradoxically, the source of not a few of his strengths and his weaknesses as a human being. This comment is offered simply to explain what are departures from details given in other biographies.

For possible errors in historical evaluation, the responsibility is wholly mine.

M.B.
Palo Alto, California
Summer, 1959

The Walls of Windy Troy

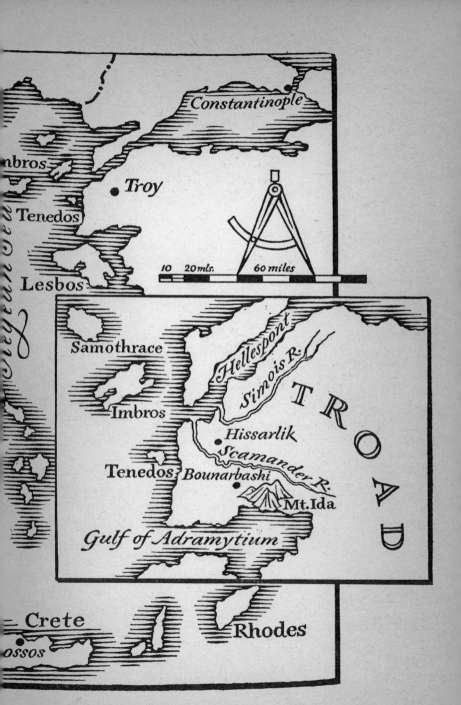

I

"That journey you have wanted so much to make
will not be postponed any longer. For I am such a
good friend of your father that I shall furnish you
with a swift ship . . ."
Athena to Telemachus. *Odyssey*, II, 285-287

The young man was nineteen, not tall for his age and
very thin. He was shifting uncomfortably from one foot
to the other, and he looked cold.

"Well," he was saying, "I know you're busy, and it's
quite a long story."

"Sit down, please," said Wendt. "I'm not that busy.
Your father was not only my teacher but my friend. What
brings you here?"

He sat down opposite the highly polished desk.
Through the wide windows behind it, he could see dozens
of sailing vessels riding at anchor in the port of Hamburg,
their canvas furled against days of departure for seaports
all over the world. Gulls flashed past the office windows
and wheeled over the docks. A wintry afternoon sun
glinted on varnished masts and spars.

"I want to go to sea," said Heinrich Schliemann.

Wendt smiled. "Most lads do. I'm surprised you didn't
decide on teaching or the ministry, though. That's more
what I'd have expected of a Schliemann." He lit a cigar.

17

"What about your father? Does he still live in Ankershagen?"

"No," said Heinrich uneasily, twisting his cap in his hands. "He's not in Ankershagen any more. I don't hear from him very often. I haven't lived at home since I was nine."

"Oh?" Wendt decided to change the subject. "Well, you must have struck out on your own early. Got plenty of ambition, have you?"

"Yes, plenty. I'm a good worker, Mr. Wendt. I've been a grocer's apprentice for nearly five years. The only thing is—"

"Yes?"

"I can't find steady work in Hamburg. I'd like—that is—"

"Look, Heinrich, maybe it would be best just to tell me why you're here, and what I can do to help you." Wendt's tone was kindly, and he was trying his best to put this tense young fellow at his ease. "It doesn't take a detective to see that you aren't eating regularly. I have no intention of grilling you. But you must be here for some reason. What is it?"

Heinrich clearly was hunting for words. "Mr. Wendt, I haven't lived at home since my mother died. That was in 1831, ten years ago."

"I'm sorry. Your mother and I came from the same little town, you know. We were childhood friends."

"Yes, I remember. Well, Father sent me and the other children to live with relatives. He—I mean, I—" Heinrich seemed to break through a barrier, for now the words came in a rush. "There was some kind of trouble. I never did get it straight. I was pretty young, anyway. It was about money. Some of the villagers claimed that Father hadn't made a proper accounting of church funds. That was while he still was the minister. I don't quite know—"

"I see. Where were you sent, Heinrich?" Wendt's brisk tone was making it easier to go on.

"I went to live with my uncle, Pastor Friederich Schliemann, in Kalkhorst. Father resigned as the minister in 1836. He thought he'd go into business. He always fancied himself a businessman, you know. The government was giving him a little pension, but money just seemed to slip away from him. It always did."

Wendt said thoughtfully, "Too bad he didn't stick to teaching. He never was a businessman. But what about you, Heinrich?"

"I went to school until I was fourteen. Uncle Friederich thought that was long enough. In his opinion a boy of fourteen was ready to do a man's work."

"And were you?"

Heinrich smiled a little shyly. "I had to be. I found a job in the village of Fürstenberg. That's about a hundred and fifty miles from here. A grocer by the name of Holtz needed an apprentice."

"Why did you leave him, Heinrich?"

"That—that's why I'm here, Mr. Wendt. I remembered my father's saying that of all his students, you had become the most successful."

"I still don't see why you're not serving out your apprenticeship. Five years is a good start on a career for a young man."

"I've always been strong, Mr. Wendt," Heinrich said.

leaning forward intently. "I'm wiry, if I'm not big. What happened is that a month ago my chest began giving me trouble. I used to work from five in the morning to eleven at night. I don't mind heavy jobs. I waited on customers and ran errands and had charge of the potato mill and the stock room until—"

"Until?"

"When I was moving barrels and casks in the stock room one morning last month, a cask of chicory got away from me and came down on my chest. I began to spit blood. For a couple of days I could hardly get out of bed."

"Did Holtz get a doctor for you?"

"Mr. Holtz was more interested in getting another apprentice. Doctors cost money."

Wendt looked at him sharply. There was no bitterness in his tone. Heinrich was simply stating facts.

"They do," Wendt agreed. "Have you been examined by anyone?"

"Oh, I'm all right now," Heinrich said quickly. "I came to Hamburg to see about starting with somebody here, but—"

"But?"

"All the Hamburg grocers seem to have what they need." He was twisting his cap again. "So I thought perhaps you might know of some ship's captain who needs a cabin boy."

Wendt puffed on his cigar and was silent. "Heinrich," he said at last, "as a ship broker it's my business to know most captains who come in and out of this port. Yes, I know a good many, but I don't know one who'd hire a cabin boy who spits blood."

"Well, I thought, sir, that a few weeks at sea—the good salt air, you know— I've been told that the best thing for chest ailments is an ocean voyage."

"That may be true. I don't know. You've been turned down by merchants here in Hamburg?"

Heinrich said reluctantly, "Yes. By five or six."

"When did you have your last meal?"

Heinrich met his eyes evenly. "I manage to eat."

The look of bleak despair told far more than Heinrich's actual words about the battle he was having to keep his nerve. He drew a large silver watch from his pocket, snapped open its case, then closed it carefully and restored it to his pocket. He rose.

"Thank you, Mr. Wendt. I'm extremely sorry to have taken your time."

"Hold on there." Wendt saw pride clashing with need, and he was touched; he would have liked to put an arm about the boy's shoulder. Stubbing out his cigar, he said, "Heinrich, don't be in such a hurry. You know that I thought a good deal of your father. Whatever he has done or has failed to do doesn't change my feeling for him. He was a good student of the classics and a good teacher. You were right to come here. But in good conscience, I can't recommend you for a cabin boy's job."

Heinrich was at the door. He was very pale. "I shall impose no longer, Mr. Wendt. It was just that you were the only businessman I knew in Hamburg—"

"Wait!" ordered Wendt, and Heinrich blinked. "You're being stiff-necked. Now you come back here and listen to a man old enough to talk to you like a father, even if you don't want to listen. No, I can't get you a berth at sea. But by heaven, I can pull some strings and get you a long sea voyage somewhere, with the chance of a decent job at the end of it. Sit down!"

"But, Mr. Wendt—"

"Be quiet. I'm going to send a clerk to get you some food. I can hear your stomach knocking against your ribs."

"But, Mr. Wendt—"

"That's enough. Do you want a job, Schliemann?"

"Yes, *sir!*"

"Then sit down and shut up."

Heinrich was soon devouring a loaf of crusty bread, a generous sausage, and steaming hot chocolate. Each time he tried to ask a question, Wendt simply pointed to the food. "Eat, just eat. I'm thinking." He began to write. One letter followed another until a small stack grew on his desk. Sounds of winches and traffic drifted up from the wharves. Wendt lit a desk lamp when early sunset tipped the masts of a hundred ships with fire.

"There," he said finally. "These are letters to businessmen I know in Venezuela."

"Venezuela!" Heinrich was startled.

"Mind you, I'm not handing you a job. Perhaps nothing will come of any of these introductions. That's up to you. Now, there's a brig called the *Dorothea* which leaves for La Guaira in a week or ten days. What you need is a change of climate. Get away from these hard northern winters here in Germany and stop pushing barrels for a while. Better," he added tersely, "stop for good. Have you any money?"

"Very little," Heinrich admitted.

Wendt picked up one of the letters. "This is to the owners of the *Dorothea*. I'm asking them, as a courtesy to me, to give you a special rate on passenger fare. Can't think why they won't; we've done business together a good many years. See them right away." The other letters he handed to Heinrich made a sizable packet. "Try them all, every last one, after you arrive. If nobody in South America can give work to an ambitious man of nineteen, I'll be surprised."

Heinrich rose. Gratitude made him suddenly formal again, but Wendt brushed aside his thanks. The broker considered adding a couple of bank notes to the letters, and his hand went tentatively to the pocket that held his billfold. But he decided against giving Heinrich money. Pride drew its boundary lines, and Wendt honored them.

"Good luck," he said heartily when they parted. As Heinrich clattered down the dark flight of stairs to the street, Wendt reflected that his old teacher's son at least had spirit and pride, if nothing else in the world.

II

"Few sons are like their fathers . . ."
Athena to Telemachus. *Odyssey*, II, 276

The *Dorothea* was a trim square-rigger built to carry passengers and cargo. To Heinrich, sitting on the dock and gazing at her while waves rippled and slapped lightly against her sides, the ship seemed impatient to be free of ropes and chains, eager to be off to sea where she belonged. And so was he, he mused, so was he. His thoughts took wing.

The ship was a symbol of the change in his luck that had started when he met Wendt yesterday. Heinrich had never quite lost faith in himself, but there had been trying days and weeks of doubt. Now his courage was strong again. The dream he cherished so secretly that he would tell no one about it was renewing its hold on him.

Pride had made him abrupt and laconic with Wendt, but pride was the guardian of his dream. No matter how badly things might go—and this past year how could they have gone worse? —he would not surrender the dream. If he were to talk about it, that would invite ridicule and he never liked to be laughed at.

One look at the shabby youth in country hand-me-down clothes was enough to make anyone dubious that he could be on his way to adventure and fame. He looked what he was, an unemployed grocer's apprentice, poorly fed and down at heel, penniless and with no strong family ties. But his destiny was to find buried cities and lost treasures in the dust of fallen empires.

Wendt must have guessed what an effort it took for Heinrich to go hat in hand and beg a favor. Wendt also may have sensed that there were things about himself and his ambitions that Heinrich carefully left unsaid. Obviously, he did not like to talk about his father.

Heinrich's early separation from home and the little gusts of scandal that had blown around his father's name had made him determined to forge an entirely different career for himself. He had reached a stern verdict: his father was a misfit and a failure. Too severe a judgment, perhaps, but he was young and he put great expectations upon himself; he was determined that no one should be able to say about him, "Like father, like son."

The minister had passed along to Heinrich, the ablest of his three sons, his own love of learning. But that was all. The pastor stayed with nothing—neither the ministry, teaching, nor business—long enough to root himself in a community or hold its respect. Yet he still tried to dictate to his grown sons and their four sisters! Heinrich had cut his ties ruthlessly. He no longer wrote his father to report where he was or what he was doing. He would prove himself first. This was an urgent need that had hardened into iron resolve.

He wondered what his father might say if he knew that at this instant he was sitting on a jetty in Hamburg, waiting for the *Dorothea*'s captain. This morning he had taken

Wendt's note to her owners. They had told him, pleasantly enough, that the final decision on price and sailing date was up to Captain Simonsen, her master. Heinrich pulled his overcoat closer and blew on his fingers; the mid-November wind off the river had a bite to it.

When I come back, I shall be a success, he thought. Not till then would he look up his family. But he felt anxiety nibbling away again: suppose Simonsen named an outlandish price? Suppose the passenger list was full? Either possibility was so alarming that Heinrich hugged his knees and fought off panic. He *had* to sail! Only with a sea voyage could he get well again, and South America promised to be the place to start his real career.

Something was delaying the captain, and the longer Heinrich waited, the more edgy he felt. Things *must* go right for him! He went back in memory to his father's study, to a Christmas when he was—let's see, seven or eight? Eight years old, he decided. His mother was still alive. He remembered her soft, pretty features only dimly; she was so gentle, so self-effacing that his father's strong presence, which towered over everything in his past, clouded her image. She had left them in death as shyly and wistfully as she had moved among them, more the spirit of a woman than flesh and blood. The hurt of being sent from home was worse for him than her actual death.

Impressions of that Christmas Day came flooding back. He could smell goose cooking in the big range, but the floor of the study where he sat was cold. Everything about the morning returned to him, for this was the day his plan —his dream—had taken hold of him. There was a book open on his lap, and its pictures were engraved forever on his mind's eye. Even now he could see those etchings of cities in ancient Egypt and Greece, and one in particular, the Scaean Gate of Troy. He remembered looking up to ask his father, "Was this the gate they dragged the Trojan horse through?"

"It is all imaginary," the pastor replied. "No one really knows what Troy was like."

"But, Father, here's a drawing of it!"

"Only an artist's idea, Heinrich. Most people agree that if there ever was a Troy, it has been in ruins for so long that nobody could tell what it was like, much less where it stood."

"But, Father—" He remembered how he had wanted to argue, and the pastor said firmly, "Many historians think that Troy was a myth, like the story of its war with the Greeks."

With these words an unreasonable, sharp feeling of being cheated had come over him.

"Then why did they put a picture of it in a history book? Why *pretend* about the gate, if all the rest is made up?"

"My son," said the pastor, "the story of the Trojan War is a legend. Poets and singers invented it for audiences who loved heroic tales. The historians who do believe that there was a Troy are certain that its remains will never be found. From everything we know it seems that the *Iliad* is a wonderful story about a war and a city that did not exist—except in Homer's poetry."

"I'll find out for myself. When I grow up, I'm going to find Troy," Heinrich had replied. His father had smiled. It sounded like a child's boasting. But the desire had grown into the fabric of his will. He had longed to continue school, to learn more history and to study Greek so that one day he could prove his belief in the existence of the real Troy. Even the dreary years of drudgery in the grocer's shop could not shake this dream.

"You're Schliemann, I take it?"

A big, rumbling voice wrenched him back to the present. The man facing him in a captain's uniform was red-faced and stocky, and he eyed Heinrich curiously. "Are you the lad wants passage?"

"My name is Schliemann," said Heinrich, mustering his dignity. "I would like to know the price and the date we sail."

With a single sweeping glance the captain took in his patched elbows and the hole in the toe of one scuffed boot. Heinrich felt his face burning.

"My owners say to fix you up," said the captain, shrugging. "We'll say—fifty marks."

Though Heinrich knew it was exactly half the going rate, the figure seemed astronomical.

"I'll get the money."

"We sail on the twenty-eighth. Passengers bring their own bedding. We don't go in for frills aboard the *Dorothea*."

"I'll have bedding," Heinrich said, and turned to leave.

"Also," Simonsen added drily, "you'll need plenty of warm clothes. The North Sea's chilly this time of year."

"Of course," Heinrich said, trying to sound casual. He left the captain staring after him rather sourly. Probably the man expected never to see hide nor hair of him again. What a surprise was in store for him, Heinrich thought.

And he began to whistle as he elbowed his way importantly past dock hands loading cargo into the holds of clippers and brigantines. What were a blanket and a few pieces of clothing to a man with a plan like his? Let the captain stare! In five or ten years he'd be staring at this Schliemann, if he got the chance, for a very different reason! He'd be telling people someday, "Yes, I remember the first time I saw him there on the Hamburg dock. Looked like a nobody, all right. Whoever would have thought—?"

Heinrich felt good, very good, for the first time in months. He braced his shoulders against the wind blowing off the Elbe, and he walked jauntily down the street in search of a pawnshop. The silver watch he had owned since childhood would be worth cash and possibly a blanket too.

He was Heinrich Schliemann! He owned a silver watch, and he had a plan. No lack of money or clothes or health or anything else could stop him now. Let people stare! How could they know he had made up his mind to be the man who found Troy?

III

"I for one say that there is nothing worse than the sea
to confuse a man, even though he may be strong."
Laodamas, to the guests. *Odyssey*, VIII, 138-139

This voyage of the *Dorothea* began smoothly enough.
Heinrich climbed aboard trying to conceal his excitement. The little ship was sturdy and sleek with new paint.
He inspected everything from stem to stern on a tour that
did little to endear him to the busy crew. He got under-
foot and was roundly sworn at, but not until he had seen
every inch of the ship did he look for his own berth. This
found, Heinrich stowed away the sum total of his worldly
possessions: a blanket, a battered second-hand Spanish
grammar, and a tin box that had seen better days. Now he
went back on deck to prop his elbows on the rail and
watch the crewmen make ready to sail.

It was nippy, this November morning of 1841. An over-
cast sky held the hint of snow. Automatically Heinrich
reached into his pocket for the watch, then grinned sheep-
ishly. The pawnbroker had known a good thing when he
saw it. He was honest enough. He had paid cash for the
old silver turnip, fifty-five marks. The decision about the
coat hadn't been easy. Heinrich had been forced to choose
between keeping his heavy wool topcoat, frayed as it was,

and exchanging it for a blanket. He reasoned that somebody might lend him a spare coat, but a blanket would be
harder to come by. So down went the coat along with the
watch and a couple of mended shirts that weren't warm
enough to wear at sea anyway. And he had walked out of
the shop with cash enough for his fare and a few coins left
over to jingle in his pocket. In an unforeseen burst of
generosity the broker had thrown in the old tin box, which
would be fine for safeguarding those precious letters of
recommendation. Besides that it held very little—the last
of the seedy shirts and a few knee-length wool stockings.

He had got his boots mended instead of buying a new
pair. He'd found the Spanish grammar in a bookseller's
stall, and the instant he saw it he knew in a flash that he
ought to learn this language since it was spoken in Venezuela. As easily and as finally as that his decision was made.

The last of the cargo was now aboard. Captain Simonsen came striding up the gangplank on his way to the pilot-
house while the dock hands cast off the hawsers. Heinrich
turned away from the rail and began patrolling the decks
as though he owned them. He made a mental promise to
himself: by the time they reached La Guaira, he would
know how to speak Spanish. To be a master of men, one
has to master their languages. Language was the key to
business success, international business such as he would
engage in. Yes, to be a master of men, he reflected, master
their languages. That sounded like something the wily
Odysseus might have said. Heinrich admired the legendary
hero and seafarer. Well, it was excellent advice, whether
he or Odysseus had thought it up.

Bells were clanging and the air rang with shouts and

orders. Ships tied up alongside seemed to be moving, so he knew the *Dorothea* was at last under way. She picked her way smoothly through the teeming harbor traffic. Heinrich took his last look at the city. He had come here in desperation. He was leaving with a deeply satisfying sense of being launched on his rightful career. His nose wrinkled happily: why, the air was salty!

For a few hours an easy wind sent the little two-master steadily along the river. Then without warning a storm began to blow. Captain Simonsen gave orders to reef sail. But the weather failed to clear and they had to tie up near the mouth of the Elbe for three days and wait for the wind to change. Heinrich disciplined his impatience by studying the lessons in his Spanish grammar. He was grappling with irregular verbs in chapter twelve by the time they were under way again. When they left the shelter of the river, the North Sea was a steely gray expanse with heaving swells. They were no sooner at sea than the wind obstinately swung around again. Just off the coast of Helgoland it veered fiercely to the west, forcing the ship to tack continually and making them lose whatever they gained in a day's run. It was obvious that the crossing was going to take much longer than usual.

Fewer than a dozen passengers were aboard. When they were scarcely a week out, Heinrich discovered that all of them were timid and some of them badly frightened. Miserable with the numbing cold and seasickness, one of the men predicted disaster. "We'll never make it," he said gloomily. "No ship built could stand up in this weather."

Heinrich refused to listen. He forced himself to keep his eyes glued on Spanish nouns and verbs. When the banshee winds failed to drown out the voice of doom, he began to read his conversation lessons at the top of his voice. He propped himself in his berth and gave himself over to learning Spanish with a noisy intensity that made his fellow passengers think him slightly daft.

Fear spread like an infection. One of the passengers announced that they ought to turn back immediately, and he made his way to Captain Simonsen across a deck awash with heavy seas. Heinrich had come out for a breath of air. He could hear the two men arguing above the whine of the wind and the drenching spray.

"Of course there's no turning back!" Simonsen yelled. "Only a fool could suggest anything so stupid. With a wind like this at our back, running free would be madness."

The passenger waved his arms and went on shouting his protests while Simonsen, his greatcoat swirling about him, clung to the rail with both hands. He bellowed furiously, "I remind you, sir, that I am captain of this ship!" The passenger gave up and staggered wretchedly to his bunk. There was no more talk of turning back.

The wind did not change quarter, but they began to gain a trifle. By the eleventh of December they could dare to believe they had ridden out the storm.

After only a few hours of blessed calm a new storm pounced upon them. The most experienced seaman aboard growled that he had seen nothing like it in his lifetime. The *Dorothea* sprang leaks. She was too small a vessel to take such punishment, and her pumps worked night and day. The passengers were hurled about in their berths, for the ship pitched violently when she mounted the swells, then slid sickeningly into their troughs. She was far off course; she had been for a couple of days.

On the morning of the twelfth, when dawn had begun to streak the sky, above the creak of rigging and the slap of torn canvas came a command: "All hands on deck! Ready the lifeboats."

Captain Simonsen seemed to be everywhere at once— piloting passengers toward the lifeboats, barking curt orders, bolstering the courage of the terrified group that huddled together on the slanting deck. Heinrich clutched his tin box in both arms and obeyed with a pounding heart. His clothes were drenched, even though he had wrapped the blanket Indian fashion about him.

The *Dorothea* had run aground on a treacherous sand bar near the island of Texel, off the Netherlands coast. She was listing crazily.

Monstrous waves swept first one and then a second lifeboat from the hands of the crew who fought savagely to launch them. Two seamen vanished from sight when another wave burst over the deck. Only after all the others were safe in the third boat did Simonsen climb in.

Heinrich had jumped into the ship's boat an instant ahead of the captain. It swayed and tossed like a chip in a mountain torrent, so that he was thrown violently off balance. The tin box shot from his arms and fell into the water, just beyond his reach. He made a grab for it, but the captain caught him and pulled him back into the boat with a fierce jerk. His eyes wide with dismay, Heinrich watched his box disappear into the water.

He dropped down wearily and tried to close his mind to the thought of all he had lost. But he could not blot out the picture of the little box sliding into the sea's wastes. The sea that was his friend, that was to have borne him and his letters to a new beginning, had become a traitorous thief.

For hours their boat was thrown about like a toy. The last of daylight was fading before they could faintly make out the shape of a barren coast. But a new horror came over them: they were helpless in the maw of the breakers, and they were being swept headlong toward the shore. Their oars and rudder were useless.

Heinrich heard a snatch of prayer and a senseless laugh, though for the most part the men were silent while the breakers rushed them forward. He could dimly see a sandy beach beyond the rocks, but even as he braced his body, he told himself they would never get through. The breakers would swallow them first. He could feel the huge combers thrust them relentlessly on. Then came the shock of impact as they struck. He was tossed like a fish from a basket into the rolling surf. The water stripped his blanket from him. He thrashed his arms and legs and was struggling for a toehold on the bottom when another breaker caught him. One foot touched sand. Then as if playing with him, the combers snatched him and whirled him over and over, head over heels. He fought for air. The last thought in his conscious mind was that the sea demanded all he had—even his life. Vast nothingness blacked out the world.

IV

"All his flesh was swollen and the seawater gushed up through his mouth and nose. He lay breathless and speechless, too tired to move, and a terrible weariness overpowered him."
Homer, of Odysseus. *Odyssey*, V, 455-457

For a long while the blackness held him. Slowly a few nightmare impressions began to break through. He was back in the grocery. He was pushing, hauling, tugging at a huge cask. It began to roll toward him. He couldn't breathe, pinned there against the wall. Customers were screaming for him and a frightful storm was raging, and old Mrs. Schneider was complaining about how slow he was. . . .

Then somehow he managed to free himself and he was alone, sweeping the empty shop. The door swung open. A young student came in bellowing, "Whisky!" and banged his fist on the counter. "Hurry up with my bottle, Heinrich."

He rushed down to the cellar where they made the cheap drink from potatoes. Back to the shop with a bottle. The student had climbed on a barrel and was chanting some verses in a language strange to Heinrich's ears. "What's that?" he asked. He kept hearing the word "Achilles," though the rest meant nothing.

The scene kept coming into proper focus. The face of

the student was clear now, and he was wagging a finger at Heinrich, saying, "I'll tell you something. The professor of Greek was so jealous of the way I recited Homer that he had me booted from the university. And my father thinks I drink too much, so he's apprenticing me to a miller."

"Homer? That's Greek you're reciting?"

"The *Iliad*, no less. Book—um—six—twelve—oh, who cares? It's all great stuff." And he went on chanting what seemed to Heinrich the most beautiful sounds he had ever heard. Now he seemed to be hearing these sounds again—music with the cadence and swing of the sea in it, language like the beat of armies surging across grassy plains. He kept the student reciting and drinking until the man begged off and made his way unsteadily into the dark street. That was when Heinrich knew he must learn Greek! The discoverer of Troy would have to know Greek as well as he knew his own tongue. He'd learn it! He'd find a tutor if he had to walk to nearby towns to get lessons. He would start right away, tonight. . . .

The scene swam out of focus. Now he was much younger, standing with a frightened little girl in the village graveyard at Ankershagen. He was prodding the moss-covered ground with a stick.

"Oh, Heinrich," the girl was saying. "I'm scared. What if the old robber knight can hear you down there in his grave? People say he can!"

"Ach," Heinrich heard himself answering, "I've often come here, and I've never seen a leg growing out of this grave."

"Then you don't believe the story?" asked Minna.

"I don't doubt that the wicked robber knight is buried

here," said Heinrich, "but I can't understand why so many people say they've actually seen his leg growing out of the ground."

Minna shuddered. "Nobody's ever seen the Maiden of the Silver Chalice, either," she said, "but everybody knows that her ghost lives in the little lake behind your house."

Heinrich stepped back. What was that, a toe? Minna let out a shriek and turned to run. Every child in Ankershagen knew the story of the evil knight whose leg, they whispered, never stopped growing, though he had been in his tomb for centuries.

"Minna, don't go!" Heinrich cried, but she was gone, and he too took to his heels, running and running, because over his shoulder he thought he saw one leg, and then another sprout from the ground. Then he stood stock still in horror, for a man's body began to heave itself clumsily from the grave. It was plodding toward him.

"Minna! Oh, Minna!" Heinrich was chasing her uphill and calling to her among the ruins of the old castle where the murderer used to hide in his lifetime.

"Minna!" The ruins echoed and re-echoed his cry until he clapped his hands over his ringing ears to shut out the noise. He heard a tapping. Ah, there she was!

"I've found the treasure, Heinrich!" she called. "But the walls are six feet thick. Come help me! We'll be rich when we find the knight's buried treasure. Then we can go and hunt for Troy together."

The wall resisted him. He tore at it and he scratched at it until chunks of rock broke off in his hands. "Minna," he promised, "we'll be rich. I'll marry you and we'll start for Troy right away."

Then, painfully, his eyes opened. His fingers were curled around pebbles and wet sand, and he was lying face down on a beach. Heinrich turned over and groaned. He pulled himself upright and spat gritty sand from his mouth. He seemed to be in one piece! He managed to stand up. He ached from his heels to the roots of his sopping hair, which was crusted with salt. What had become of his boots? He was barefoot.

Far off across the dunes he could see a little cluster of men, and one of them began to run toward him.

The nightmare visions of the hours he had sprawled unconscious on the sand were still so vivid that he had to struggle to get his grip on reality. He was not back in the folklore-haunted town of his boyhood. He was not the grocer's apprentice waiting on a drunken student. That man (heavens, he could even remember his name—Hermann Niederhöffer!) seemed as real as he had been the night Heinrich had listened to him recite Homer. And because he was weak and confused, it seemed to him that Minna, his childhood playmate, must still be somewhere nearby. He had seen her for the last time when she was fourteen. He knew then she was really his girl. He was planning to write and ask her to wait for him, just as soon as he could. Minna was the only person in the world who knew of his dream about Troy. She was the only one who would not laugh at him for it. As a boy he'd said he would marry her. And he meant to. He still meant to.

The running figure was coming closer. Heinrich tried to shout something, then winced, because his mouth hurt. No wonder! Two teeth were broken. Through the rips in his shirt he could see that his skin was mottled with bruises.

But there was one undeniable fact: he was alive, and that was a great surprise.

Athena was the goddess who had stood at Odysseus' side to help him through all his trials. Gray-eyed Athena must be standing by Schliemann! He had to smile, though even smiling hurt. He was as lucky as Odysseus, who had been shipwrecked and saved he didn't know how many times. Schliemann and Odysseus, the shipwrecked adventurers!

The running figure was waving at him, and Heinrich straightened up to return a salute that was almost jaunty.

V

"But since you have come here to our city and country, you shall not lack for clothes or for any other thing that is due a sorely tried castaway who asks us for help."
Nausicaä to Odysseus. *Odyssey*, VI, 191-193

Nothing that happened to Odysseus was any more miraculous than this. Except for the two men washed overboard, every one of the *Dorothea*'s passengers and crew was alive, carried ashore onto a great sandbank just off the Dutch island of Texel.

The friendly fisherman who had found them led the way as they waded and limped through the sands to firmer coastal ground. Here he had a wagon in which he drove them to his own cottage. He quickly got a roaring fire going, and as they huddled about it, gave them strong hot coffee and hunks of brown bread. They ate ravenously. Then the exhausted and tattered men fell asleep anywhere possible, several of them on the floor.

They soon learned that there was a German consulate not far distant in one of the island's small villages, and from this man they could expect assistance in returning to Hamburg. Heinrich was the only member of the weather-beaten lot who had nothing to chip in when Captain Simonsen suggested they pool whatever money they had managed to bring ashore to pay at least a part of the cost of return passage. Heinrich ruefully pulled his pockets inside out to display their emptiness.

"Too bad, Jonah," said Simonsen. "But don't worry your head about it. The consul will fix us up." The captain was counting the collection when the Dutch fisherman who was their rescuer came in with something in his hands.

"My tin box!" Heinrich shouted. Simonsen translated the man's explanation. News of the shipwreck had spread quickly among the islanders. One of them had just found the box, which had been cast up on the bank not far from where Heinrich himself came ashore.

"You may be a Jonah," said Simonsen, and Heinrich saw that he was grinning, "but maybe your luck is changing." The letters of recommendation inside the box were bone dry, and so were Heinrich's few clothes. How he needed them!

"When I first laid eyes on you," the captain told him, "I said to myself, 'Now this one's a Jonah. Looks like a sick cat and may die on my hands.' Look at you now! Sick? Nothing like a first-rate shipwreck to build you up." He clapped a hand on Heinrich's shoulder. "How about it? I've lost everything, and I have to go back and face the owners to explain the loss of my ship. Every other man jack aboard lost the shirt off his back. But the worst you can say is that you got ashore minus your boots and a couple of teeth." He chuckled. Simonsen was much more of a human being on land than he had seemed at sea. "Guess you need more luck than the rest of us, Jonah, so I don't begrudge it to you."

Wearing a pair of borrowed wooden shoes, a gift to him

from the fisherman, Heinrich walked with his companions to the village where the consul was located. The tin box went along under his arm; it had become his lucky piece, and he would not let it out of his sight.

The consul assured them they would all be returned to Hamburg; a packet boat was leaving within twenty-four hours. As the men rested and doctored one another's cuts and bruises, Heinrich kept silent and to himself. Finally he asked to speak to the consul privately. "I would rather not return to Germany," he announced firmly. "I want to go to Amsterdam instead."

"Extraordinary!" said the official, a man to whom this seemed a breach of orderly routine. "I should think you'd want to get back to your own country after this terrible experience."

"Well, there's not only the problem of money," Heinrich admitted, "but—" and he briefly explained his illness, the futile hunt for work in Hamburg, the kindness of Wendt. "Something tells me I belong in Holland. I haven't a pfennig to my name, and I discovered that there were no jobs for me in Hamburg. It might be different in Amsterdam."

Seeing it useless to argue with this determined young man in the threadbare clothes and the clumsy wooden shoes, the consul gave in. He insisted that Heinrich accept some money, and although Heinrich felt rather like a man receiving alms, he took it. The consul also provided Heinrich with a letter to another consul in Amsterdam. While the other survivors and Captain Simonsen went back to Hamburg, Heinrich followed his independent course to Amsterdam, his passage on a small packet boat paid by the consul. On the way he wrote a letter to Wendt, in Hamburg, reporting his adventurous voyage in detail.

In Amsterdam began the hunt for work. Heinrich lived frugally on the consul's money in as cheap a room as he could find. Occasional odd jobs made it possible to buy a respectable suit and new boots. But it was a struggle to keep up his spirits. There seemed to be no steady job for him.

He had quite forgotten about his letter to Wendt by the time a reply came. Wendt wrote that he had received Heinrich's news on a day when he was going to dine with friends. Heinrich's account of the shipwreck made such a dramatic tale that he had taken the letter with him to read to them. On the spur of the moment he and his friends had decided to send money to the plucky German lad who had courage enough to strike out on his own instead of coming back to ask Wendt for further help. With characteristic thoughtfulness, Wendt enclosed some letters of recommendation to businessmen in Amsterdam along with a generous bank draft.

It was through this good friend, then, that Heinrich was referred to a merchant who needed an errand boy, and it was Wendt he could thank when he got the job. What did he do? Among other things, he stamped bills of exchange, took them to banks to be cashed, and carried letters to and from the post office. The work kept him in the open air most of the day. Thank heaven there were no crates or barrels that needed the strength of an ox to handle. He told himself that this job could have a future, just as big a future as he wanted. Not in running errands, of course. But doing such simple leg work gave Heinrich time to think his own

thoughts. While his legs ran the pavements, the best possible way to occupy his mind, he decided, was to learn
languages. He had a good start on Spanish. He must learn
Dutch right away, obviously, and he soon would need
English and French. And, as every ambitious businessman
knew, he would need Russian, too. He would have to resist the temptation to learn Greek, a tongue he had wanted
to master ever since the tipsy student had recited Homer
to him. Greek could wait. First must come the languages
needed for tools. Before long he would convince his employer that he was absolutely indispensible. He would be
promoted to better and more responsible positions in Mr.
Quien's business. From errand boy to clerk to junior part-
ner to . . .

Come to think of it, it shouldn't take *too* many years to
scrape together the amount of money he would need before he could start his expedition to search for Troy. If
he wasted no time at all, saved and used every hour, every
minute, it might take less than ten years.

He must buy an English dictionary with his first wages.
And write Minna. His future wife should know what had
been happening to him. No doubt about it, he thought, the
sea voyage had restored his health. He felt wonderfully
well, and he fairly sprinted through the streets of Amsterdam, as much at home in the big friendly city as if he had
been born there. There was certainly much to be said for
the salt-air treatment for a weak chest. If you survived the
voyage, that is!

VI

"He saw the cities of many men whose ways he learned . . ."

Homer, of Odysseus. *Odyssey*, I, 3

"I beg your pardon, sir." Heinrich faced a surprised gentleman whose hat had gone sailing into the gutter when they collided. "*Je vous prie pardon. Excusez-moi.*"

The passer-by looked more puzzled than ruffled.

"I was trying to think of the French word for 'business.' I should have watched where I was going." The serious-faced, sandy-haired errand boy dusted off the hat and stood holding it absent-mindedly while he searched his memory. "Ach! *Les affaires*, of course." He bowed. "Thank you. Excuse me again, sir. Good day." He patted his pocket to make sure his papers were safe, reopened his French drill book, and raced down the street, his head bent over the book as it had been before the collision. The man gazed after him openmouthed.

"*Les affaires de mon cousin sont, sont—*"

At the bank Heinrich marched briskly to the teller's window. "*Donnez-moi, s'il vous plaît, deux cent vingt-huit*—no, that's wrong. I mean, *deux cent vingt—*"

"What is it now, young man?" The teller's snappish tone brought him down to earth. "Don't practice that *parlez-vous* stuff on me. Save it for your boss if he's crazy enough to put up with it. Now, in good honest Dutch, what is it you want today?"

People in Amsterdam's business district were getting used to the sight of Mynheer Quien's studious office boy running the streets with his nose forever in a book. But there was consternation the first Sunday Heinrich went to the church attended by English-speaking residents of the city. The slender, neatly dressed young man in the pew nearest the pulpit sat talking to himself quite audibly throughout the service. Suddenly he noticed that everyone around him was scowling, and he was obliged to move to a back pew when an indignant British woman leaned over to whisper, "If *you're* preaching today, why don't you take the pulpit?"

He had to content himself with a back seat, which was a pity because he could hardly hear. He was merely getting used to the sound of spoken English, training his tongue to repeat the sounds; he hadn't the faintest notion what the words meant.

Soon he was reading English novels, always aloud, always in full voice, without stopping to translate. He had discovered this to be a more efficient system than studying grammar. Words and sounds and meanings made connections in his head, and he gradually got the sense of what he was reading.

He developed this method because he couldn't afford lessons with a professional teacher—at least, not nearly so often as he wanted. Occasionally he hired someone to read and correct the letters and the schoolboyish essays he wrote in the new language.

He studied while he waited his turn in line at bank and

post office. He studied as he ate his lunch and ran errands. In six months, with some help from a tutor when he could afford one, he learned English. New languages came to him as naturally as breathing. He had known this about himself when he was eight, reading Latin with his father, and when he was thirteen his skill had delighted his teacher, Carl Andres, back in Kalkhorst. Andres had told him, "You could be a linguist if you wanted, Heinrich. I've never seen a boy read and translate as you do."

He kept his Spanish from growing rusty while he added English and French to his kit of master tools. He scurried importantly around Amsterdam with a book in his hand and ears pricked up like a young colt's, listening for the chatter of French or Spanish or English, and he would burst joyously into a stranger's conversation for the sake of practice.

There were ample opportunities to meet people and observe the men and women of a cosmopolitan city. What he saw and heard was making him critical of the way he spoke his mother tongue. Measuring his vocabulary against those of more worldly people, he had to confess that it was a country boy's and that he made ignorant mistakes in grammar.

To correct this, he mapped out a strict schedule of reading. Night after night in the little attic room that was the best housing he could afford, he read English and French and the masterpieces of his German heritage. His breakfast was rye-meal porridge. Dinner was something hot and stomach-filling and cheap. True nourishment came from words and ideas. Grasping the meaning of a page in French gave him the sort of exhilaration that comes to another man from a glass of champagne. Sometimes he got drunk with words—French, English, Spanish, and new German words.

He was soon the master of five languages, because he acquired Dutch as a matter of routine. The excitement of mastery made him indifferent to fatigue or illness. The curious fact was that he never had been so well. He had come to the conclusion that nothing worse than a broken blood vessel in his chest had caused his blood-spitting last year. He was keyed up by growing self-discovery. At last he was gaining a little of the education denied him during his hard-driven youth.

Most of what he earned—and it was about $160 a year—went into books: grammars, dictionaries, and the writings of famous authors. To his other languages Heinrich soon added Italian and Portuguese. He spent money for lessons with a famous teacher of handwriting, knowing that a beautiful copperplate hand would increase his value as a clerk.

By some means Heinrich couldn't quite explain, his father found out where he was. Letters begging for money began to pester him. The elder Schliemann was without a shred of pride. Heinrich wanted to ignore the letters, but duty was a stern taskmaster. He squeezed something now and then from his wages and sent it back to Germany, each time feeling a twinge of disgust, and each time resolving to be as unlike his father as his will and youth *and money* could make him.

Even if Heinrich had gone to a university, he could scarcely have absorbed any more learning than he made his own in the fast-moving years from 1841 to 1844. By the time he was twenty-three he understood that his memory could be disciplined and used as he required. He was finding out how to make use of it with the calculated finesse of an athlete building up his legs and his lungs for track. He was pushing himself deliberately and tirelessly to be a successful businessman. The eventual goal was the discovery of Troy. He was marching on his way. Each time his wages increased, he felt that he had moved a few steps farther. It would take money to be an excavator. It would take money to realize his dream. Very well, he would put his mind, his heart, his energies into making money.

The years flew by. Whatever had sapped his strength before, assuredly it had not been tuberculosis. He had boundless vitality. When he could feel that today's work was creating tomorrow's opportunities, he was buoyant with optimism. When he had no new subject to challenge him, and when too many stagnant, unaccounted-for minutes were left over from the day's activities, he was restless and irritable.

"Mr. Quien," he said to his employer one morning, "I've been studying bookkeeping."

"Good for you," said Quien, a quiet-spoken man intent on a ledger.

"And perhaps you've noticed the change in my handwriting?"

"Can't say that I have, Heinrich. I've so many other things to notice."

Heinrich tried a different tack. "What I'm really asking is whether you are ready to promote me. I have prepared myself to be an efficient clerk."

"I've plenty of clerks, Heinrich. What I do need is a reliable errand boy. Have you been to the bank yet?"

Heinrich reflected that he might have been too good an errand boy. They parted on friendly terms. He was ready for bigger things.

In 1844 the firm of B. H. Schröder and Company hired him as a copy clerk, or correspondent. There was some bookkeeping to do. This prosperous firm with far-flung international connections offered him a chance to prove himself. He was challenged. He kept his eyes and ears open. Acquiring Russian would be a good investment. The Schröder firm transacted business with many merchants in St. Petersburg.

He looked around Amsterdam for a tutor, but the only person who knew the language was the Russian vice-consul. Heinrich appeared one day in his office and went straight to the point. "I wonder whether you could find a few hours a week to give me lessons in Russian?"

"Russian lessons? My dear sir, I'm not a teacher."

"But you speak Russian, and I want to learn it. I'm sure we could work out an agreeable financial arrangement—"

The consul, to Heinrich's regret, coolly declined. How very inconvenient! He had to fall back on his more tedious system of self-instruction.

Since he made better progress if he had someone—anyone—to whom he could read, he hired a poverty-stricken Dutch student, who knew not a single word of any language except his own, to sit in his room evenings and listen to him read what they both devoutly hoped was Russian. Heinrich picked up the pronunciation from a grammar, then graduated immediately to novels. "Wake up! Sit up there!" he would command sharply whenever the student closed his drooping eyes. His voice would rise to a resounding shout if the listener dozed off.

"I'm not paying you to sleep," he said impatiently. "Listen efficiently, will you? Earn your money!"

When he came to a particularly difficult passage, he wrestled with it at the top of his lungs. This was helpful, he thought, in covering up mistakes.

He had to move from two different rooming houses. Landladies raised the most unreasonable objections to the way he studied!

The day came when he could compose his first letter for the firm. Mr. Schröder was gratified. "I wasn't aware when I hired you that you knew Russian, my boy."

"I didn't."

Schröder, who liked his employees to have initiative, was even more impressed to learn about the other languages. This young German was not only adaptable and ambitious, he was a linguistic wizard.

"Two of our most important clients are arriving next week from St. Petersburg, Heinrich. I had planned to hire a translator, but maybe you would like to take over the interview. I'll find a way to express my thanks if you do well and close the deal."

"I am honored, sir. Of course I shall."

Schröder had no further need for hired translators. In January of 1846 he named Heinrich the firm's representative in St. Petersburg.

Heinrich was twenty-four and this appointment represented a success. But it was not enough, not nearly enough. While he packed his valises with custom-made shirts and suits from Amsterdam's best British tailor, he took careful stock of how far he had progressed and where he was going. He was merely at the outset of his career. Once he was settled in St. Petersburg he would write to Minna. The dream cherished for sixteen years, through stormy poverty and hopes often shipwrecked, was not too far from realization. Marrying Minna was the next logical step in it.

"Dearest Minna," he began, composing the lines in his head as he packed, "My esteemed Minna . . . Minna, my dear one. . . ." He wrote and rewrote the letter a hundred different ways in his head, but eventually he decided that it was not quite time to set it down on paper.

He was every inch the young man of business when he left by ship for St. Petersburg. He was assured, polished in manner, and he could converse easily with people of many countries. He watched Amsterdam sink below the horizon, recalling one other time he had seen a city disappear behind a ship's wake. No storms that blew, no shipwreck, could delay him again. He had a timetable. He would have to defer his Greek study for no longer than another year, or at the most, two. He reminded himself to consult back files of Russian newspapers. What were the Italian excavators doing this season in the ruins of Pompeii? He had neglected to follow their new findings while he kept his nose to the grindstone of learning modern languages. Brilliant discoveries had been made there only a few years ago. The whole buried city was being reconstructed.

The days were too short for all he wanted to do, even when he rose at five and devoted the after-business hours to study. He would have to find out whether there were any new editions of Homer in English or French. He derived enormous satisfaction from the fact that the city of Troy was still undiscovered. Most Continental scholars were insisting—smugly, he thought—that it never would be found.

Heinrich Schliemann was too busy to argue with scholars. He had his own long-range plan, and it was moving along well enough to suit him. Let the graybeards dig around in the ruins of Pompeii. Let them toss their hats in the air over fresh discoveries of gladiators' bodies found in the Colosseum, over glass jars and fishermen's boats and bakers' ovens covered with volcanic ash and the rubble of ages. Very interesting. But once his fortune was made, he would give men cause to marvel at vastly older and more astonishing discoveries, perhaps the Scaean Gate. Or— who knows?—the jewels of Helen of Troy or the armor of Achilles! Meanwhile, he would work and amass money and bide his time.

VII

"Nothing more terrible than this could I suffer . . ."
Achilles to the dead Patroclus. *Iliad*, XIX, 321

When Peter the Great decided that he wanted a city close to Europe with a port on the Baltic, he picked the site of St. Petersburg. Ships could come and go most of the year on the Neva River. A city on piles arose from the marshes and deltas of this river. Peter had ways of getting what he wanted, whatever the cost in men or money. The saying was that this city was built on bones, so great was the number who had died in creating it.

The first time Heinrich went sightseeing he gazed in awe at the mighty equestrian statue of Peter. The czar's Winter Palace and the Alexander Nevsky Cathedral were buildings as grand as he ever expected to see. The Academy of Sciences drew him like a magnet. How often he had read about it! And here he was strolling through its halls!

If Heinrich truly had suffered from lung trouble, this city with its wretchedly damp climate might have been the death of him. Lying as it did so far north on the globe, its seasons reflected the Arctic in brief summer nights and long cruel winters. But weather was the last thing that concerned him.

St. Petersburg had known unrest not many years before, and revolutionary uprisings had been sternly crushed. Heinrich was aware only that St. Petersburg was the most gracious city of his experience. He did not observe the vast extremes between the very rich and the very poor. His first and foremost concern was business, and this kept him in a narrow channel, steering a course midway between the aristocrats and people of the working class. He dealt exclusively with merchants who talked and appraised and bartered and traded indigo, cotton, oil, flax, wool. In his walks around the city he might bump against begging street children, and he recalled his father's Bible maxim about the poor whom we have always with us, as he dug into his pockets for a few kopecks to hand them. The sight of the czar's entourage with its showy armed guards on prancing horses never failed to stir him, for he had been born and reared in Mecklenburg, the most conservative of all German duchies, and he tipped his hat to nobility from long habit. Politics didn't interest him. First, last, always, and even in dreams at night, his life was directed unswervingly toward success in business so that one day he could hunt the gleaming city of Troy. Whatever interfered with his business was an interruption of his timetable.

He went his way in St. Petersburg as deliberately and intensely as he did everything else. With this deliberateness he had swept Holtz's shop immaculately clean instead of doing a slovenly job. With this intensity he had taught himself five languages. Only those things were real that advanced or threatened his central plan. He liked St. Petersburg and felt at home here.

"I plan to be married very shortly," he told a friend one

day. He had written his proposal in a letter to Minna, and it was on its way to Germany. He had money enough to provide all he wanted his wife to enjoy. The rest was being saved for the future. He had been financing his brother Louis from time to time, helping him make a start on his own career in business in Amsterdam. But Louis worried him when he gave thought to the matter. In Heinrich's critical eyes he was very like their father. Louis drifted from one job to another. This year, though, he had sailed for New York. Once in a while letters came to say that he was at last doing well. The Schliemann sisters were either married or living with relatives. Paul, the youngest brother, had been killed in an accident. The family no longer required as much help of Heinrich as they had in the past when he could least afford to send them money. Pastor Schliemann himself had married again. Heinrich had fallen into the habit of sending him regular sums, a sort of pension arrangement that took care of filial obligations and was to continue until the pastor's death. His harsh attitude toward his father had somewhat softened with the years.

So Heinrich selected a tentative date for the wedding and was drawing up a guest list of his new Russian friends. Which church would be most pleasing to Minna? She would have to travel a good three weeks from Germany, assuming that the letter reached her promptly.

He was working at his desk in the waterfront office that frequently reminded him of Wendt's headquarters in Hamburg. A clerk who brought the morning mail saw him seize one letter eagerly, open it, then rise uncertainly from his chair with the note paper clutched in his hand.

"Mr. Schliemann, are you ill?"

Heinrich waved him away. "No, no. I am not sick. I've had some bad news."

"Have we lost a shipment, sir? That cargo from Alexandria is five days overdue."

"No, I tell you. Someone—an old friend—has sent news that I had not expected." One hand gripped the desk. He looked like a man in pain. The clerk watched him fold the paper and lock it away in a desk drawer. Heinrich, with his passion for neatness, made a habit of saving every document he received.

He said heavily, "I am leaving for the rest of the day." That was all. From the wall he took the silk top hat and the heavy fur greatcoat that were the winter attire of St. Petersburg's more important businessmen. Now the clerk was certain he was ill. Heinrich was the one who opened the office every morning, and his lamp usually burned until midnight.

"You are positive, sir, there is nothing I can do?"

But Heinrich was gone. He walked the streets aimlessly and lingered on the city's bridges, staring moodily into the dark water of its canals. Minna was married. She had married, the letter said, less than a year ago. The news was written with casual impersonality by a mutual friend; Minna herself did not reply.

He wandered the streets most of the night. All her life, he reminded himself, Minna had said very little. When they were children holding hands to explore the old castle in Ankershagen, and even when they had met after the long separation, both of them fourteen, Minna had said very little. He was the talker. He could not say, fairly, that she had broken her promise; she had made no promise.

The future without Minna? He blamed himself for not seeing her before he came to Russia, cursed his self-assurance for waiting until now to propose. Well, what did it matter? He turned back and headed for his office. There was always work to be done.

By the end of that first year in Russia he had established himself in his own business, and this testifies to the sort of discipline he could impose on himself. He continued to represent Schröder and Company, but he set up his own office to deal in indigo. Disappointment was buried in work and more work. Then he began to travel far and wide, ensuring the new firm's future with trips to Moscow and journeys to London, Paris, Brussels, Hamburg, Berlin, and many another European city in the next three years.

He made a meteoric rise. Everywhere he went, Heinrich was soon commanding attention as the young merchant prince that he was. He stayed only at the best hotels, where, it is true, he thriftily took the least expensive rooms. He was still young, and he was prosperous, a connoisseur of food, a versatile linguist, a man with a plan and a style of life. Until he lost her, Heinrich had not known how much he cared for Minna, and it would take time for him to recover from the feeling of loss.

In 1848 something else happened to upset his timetable. Minna's marriage to another man had been the first unforeseen event, and the second was the discovery of gold in California.

VIII

"I myself guided him that he might make a good
reputation by going to that place."
   Athena, telling Odysseus about Telemachus.
   Odyssey, XIII, 422-423

Louis Schliemann was dead. How ironic! Louis, the
ne'er-do-well brother, the restless young rover who had
tried his hand at clerking, banking, teaching, and selling,
was dead, and it seemed to Heinrich that he had only begun
to find himself.

Stories of riches being made overnight in California had
hypnotized Louis into leaving New York. He had beaten
his way west in the vanguard of the forty-niners and
reached Sacramento early enough to start reaping a golden
harvest not in the diggings, but in banking. California was a
moneylender's paradise. The interest rate on loans was
sky-high—and soaring.

Louis had set out with little money of his own, but in
letters to Heinrich he kept reporting that the stacks of
dollars were piling up. He had formed a banking partnership with another man. Heinrich read his glowing accounts
and marveled; they seemed to him more like fairy tales
than sober truth. Though at first he shook his head in dis-
belief, the reports kept coming. Heinrich was fascinated.
Louis's letters made no mention, however, of conditions in

the swarming, makeshift gold camps that had sprung up around Sacramento. Here disease struck relentlessly. Scores of men were dying of typhoid fever.

Abruptly Louis himself became ill and died of it. Heinrich got word of his death before others in the Schliemann family did. Louis had left an estate. How large or small it was no one knew, but his final letter had sounded almost delirious with excitement at the ease with which men could make money.

By this time Heinrich's firm in St. Petersburg was flourishing. He could safely leave its management to his employees. If fortunes were being made in California, that was where he belonged; he had been thinking this even before Louis died. Everything urged him on now that Louis seemed to have left an estate.

Heinrich was on board the steamer *Atlantic* in December of 1850 when she pulled out of Liverpool. His trip would have a threefold purpose: to locate his brother's grave, claim the estate, and make investments of his own, if prospects were only half as good as Louis had described them. The money Heinrich had saved and whatever he might make in America would all go someday to buy the tools and equipment an explorer needed to uncover the site of Troy. When he thought of the uses there would be for his money in terms of work gangs to hire, spades, wheelbarrows, and pickaxes to buy, he could find no argument against making the American trip. His timetable was not actually being interrupted; it simply had been changed.

A dozen times the sea voyage brought back memories of the *Dorothea*'s voyage, nine years ago. What a child he had been, he mused. Today he was one of St. Petersburg's leading businessmen. If California should prove to be his personal El Dorado, he might retire in a very short while. Strange that fate sped him on his way to ancient Troy by arranging this roundabout journey to the New World!

The sea behaved toward him as though it still were his enemy, showing him as little respect as when he was a waif. This was another stormy voyage. The *Atlantic* might be the grandest steamer in the world, as Heinrich thought she was, but she pitched and tossed, she rolled and she wallowed in westerly gales. Eighteen hundred miles out of Liverpool her engines ground to a stop. The captain hoisted sail and tried to reassure his passengers, who were nearly as frightened as those aboard the *Dorothea*. Heinrich found their nervousness rather foolish; the sea held no surprises for him. Food had to be rationed in case the storms did not ease off; then when supplies ran dangerously low and the weather was unchanging, the ship made for the nearest port, which was Queenstown (now Cobh), Ireland.

In February Heinrich set out again, now aboard the *Africa*, and good weather made the crossing uneventful. His ship reached "Zandy-hock" and entered New York harbor after only fifteen days at sea, firing off cannon and rockets to announce the safety of the *Atlantic*, which many feared lost at sea. Presses worked overtime to print the joyful news. It spread over the wires of that new marvel, the electric telegraph, to Louisiana and Mississippi and Michigan.

Heinrich made the Astor House his headquarters in New York and stayed long enough to get acquainted with the city. Its neat brick houses and paved streets pleased his critical eye, but he noted in the diary he was keeping that New York could not be compared architecturally with any of the European capitals. He visited P. T. Barnum's museum. It entertained him no more than his first minstrel show. Yankee humor was always a little beyond him. The comments he put into his diary about women proved that his interest in them was reviving. Yet the comparisons he made between American and European girls were not particularly flattering. "An over-vivacity and a very great tendency to be frivolous and amusing," he wrote soberly in his journal, "are the chief characteristic of the Yankees' daughters." He thought the weather might have something to do with this. "The quick change of the temperature," he wrote, was the reason that American girls looked "old and worn out at twenty-two."

On his way to California Heinrich paused in Washington. It was a measure of his growing prestige that he should pay a formal call on the President of the United States and be graciously received as a distinguished guest. Mr. Fillmore introduced his wife and daughter, a girl of seventeen who struck Heinrich, so he duly recorded in his diary, as looking "rather green." No doubt about it, American women drew his eye, but he was discriminating. He was also wary. His reputation as a merchant prince went with him on his travels, and Americans, who to his mind exaggerated almost all facts and figures, tended to overestimate his wealth. Actually, nothing could please him more . . . but he wasn't going to be taken in by swindlers or fooled by crooks and crackpots—least of all by designing women!

That hungry curiosity of his led Heinrich to many of

the conventional tourist spots and to out-of-the-way places as well, whether they happened to be prisons or universities. Sometimes he went alone, again with groups of sightseers. He saw the Washington Monument, which was not quite completed, and it greatly impressed him, but he was scornful of the souvenir hunters in his party when they visited Mount Vernon. A few of them pried little stones from the wall of Washington's tomb to take home with them; to Heinrich this was stupid vandalism.

In railway carriages and hotels he jotted down his observations about the bustling new cities and towns of America. The people themselves caused him feelings of admiration mingled with distaste. They were so very enthusiastic about everything and always in such a terrible hurry! He was keeping his diary in English, because it was his custom to speak and write only in the language of the country he was visiting.

In Baltimore he ate oysters for dinner and oysters for breakfast before leaving for Chagres, Panama, aboard the *Crescent City*. His boat crossed the Isthmus of Panama by way of the Chagres River as far as Gorgona. From Gorgona to the port city of Panama on the Pacific side of the Isthmus one had to travel on foot and by muleback through hot, sticky, fever-breeding country, for there was no railroad. Travelers brave enough to risk the jungle lived on food that was offensive to Heinrich's gourmet palate. In spite of himself he enjoyed the trip, though it made him furious to be overcharged for commonplace necessities. He was sure that most of the natives would cheerfully cut his throat for his luggage. Still, the country was magnificent. The adventurer in him was entirely happy.

Nothing would do but he must hire a mule when he reached Panama, to set out in the burning sun for a long ride to the ruins of the ancient city of Panama, founded during the lifetime of Cortés. The fragments of old walls and crumbled buildings enthralled him, for here was an authentic ruined city with a romantic history, and sitting astride his mule, he allowed himself to wonder how long it might be before he could start his search for a ruined city incalculably more important and imposing than this one.

By far the worst part of the journey to California was the crossing of the Isthmus. The rest of the way to San Francisco, aboard the *Oregon,* was a pleasant, relaxing experience. The *Oregon* carried live steers that the cooks butchered to provide fresh meat for the passengers.

Whenever the vessel touched a Mexican port to load or discharge passengers and cargo, Heinrich practiced his Spanish. He was having use for all the languages he knew, and he could now speak eight.

The passengers first glimpsed San Francisco as a city half concealed from view by the masts of the ships in her harbor. Eighteen months ago there had been nothing more than a village here. Today the streets, the crowded business districts, and the heavily laden docks hummed with activity.

Heinrich found a private room. He might be prosperous but he was scandalized at the prices asked by the Union Hotel—seven dollars a day for room and meals! He could certainly do without eggs at a dollar each and butter at two dollars a pound. Most foodstuffs were being shipped in from the East. Nobody in his right mind wanted to buy acreage in California to farm, because any fool knew that

California land was worthless except for mining and grazing.

Locating Louis's grave took longer than he had anticipated, but Heinrich found it after going by river boat from San Francisco to the inland town of Sacramento. Above the grave he placed a handsome marble marker. Now it was time to look into the matter of Louis's estate. If he had allowed himself any wild hopes, they would have crashed to earth. Heinrich had known his brother only too well. The few hundred dollars Louis had left were so snarled with partnership red tape that he could not claim them without going to court. The wheels of justice in this frontier community ground too slowly to suit him.

There was, then, no fortune ready-made and his for the claiming; but Louis had been right about how easy it was to make money. Gamblers, get-rich-quick artists, and swindlers had discovered that. Each incoming coach or ship brought a fresh crop of would-be prospectors. "*Dummköpfe*," Heinrich called them; idiots and dreamers, piling into California expecting to find streets lined with gold, only to become prey for the sharper with the phony mine or the crooked card game.

The businessman in him watched the bonanza seekers and pitied them, but all the while his shrewd common sense told him that there was ample opportunity here for an honest, hard-headed business enterprise.

He took his time about deciding where and how to begin. First he explored all possibilities, traveling around to boom towns and roaring camps in the Mother Lode country, and at last deciding that the best place to open his business was Sacramento. Not for Heinrich Schliemann the easy-come, easy-go schemes of speculators. He knew eight languages, and these were the tools he most needed now, exactly as he had foreseen.

Yes, poor brother Louis had been correct about one fact: fortunes could be made. Now it was Heinrich's turn.

IX

"You are the shrewdest of men, and no one else in
the world can match you."
　　　Telemachus to Odysseus. *Odyssey*, XXIII, 124-126

"If I knew fifty languages," Heinrich told his assistant
cashier, "I still couldn't talk with every man in that line in
his own tongue." He stopped his weighing and counting
long enough to gaze at the long queue of people, which
extended through the door of the bank and out into the
street.

Chinese in big straw hats and padded black jackets;
Mexicans, Chileans, and Peruvians in sun-brilliant, flaming
serapes, gaudy as birds of the jungle; unkempt and cop-
per-skinned Indians. In the same line were Italians, their
ear lobes dangling bright golden rings; Americans in top
hats, Americans in tatters, Americans in their cups, and
Americans in an all-fired hurry . . . all waiting to trade
nuggets and dust for cash money.

"Ach, why didn't I learn Chinese while I was about it?
How could I have been so lazy?"

"You, *lazy?*" exclaimed his clerk. "When was that, Mr.
Schliemann?"

"Enough," Heinrich said. "We waste time."

While footloose adventurers drank and gambled away
their strikes, Heinrich settled down methodically to bank-

ing. The largest part of the gold he collected went to the House of Rothschild, which had a San Francisco branch office. Armed messengers arrived on the nightly river boat to exchange cash for Heinrich's raw gold.

The bank soon had to be enlarged. Heinrich went about town armed with Colt "revolving pistols" and carried a vicious-looking bowie knife in his belt. Bank robberies were frequent. He knew restless nights when he lay awake worrying over the loss of his life or his gold, and he missed his beloved St. Petersburg, where the czar's law and order made it possible for a man to go outside without fear of being stabbed or clubbed for his money.

By and large, however, Heinrich admitted to himself that he liked America. He had to respect the boundless energy and industry of her people. He only wished that not so many of them were given to sharp practices. To a countryman visiting the bank he said one day, his hand on a pile of money sacks, "These Americans! They seem to be dedicated to nothing so much as the making of money!" The flicker of a smile appeared on his friend's face. Heinrich interpreted it as courteous agreement.

Business took him to the towns of Grass Valley, Rough & Ready, and Nevada City. His hotel was often a canvas tent. With gusto and with pride the reputation of the West for being wild and woolly was noisily justified in places like these.

One June night in 1851 he was asleep in a San Francisco hotel when a cry of fire roused him. He bolted to the street and moved along with a crowd that was streaming up Telegraph Hill. It was from this height that he watched the spectacle of a city in flames. Demolition squads fought the fire's spread by blowing up iron and wooden buildings in its path, but by morning the town appeared to be a total loss. And then the speed with which San Franciscans turned to and began immediately to rebuild gave Heinrich his final estimate of Americans as a people who were the most resourceful of men—except, of course, the Germans, and possibly the Russians.

Despite a few anxious moments, all was going so well that Heinrich might have stayed longer in California. But fever hit him, too. His doctor warned him sternly that he was not likely to survive a second attack. As Heinrich recorded in his journal, he was afraid that the climate of Sacramento was poisonous to him. He accepted the current scientific theory that the intense heat of summer in this valley town caused animal and vegetable matter in outlying swamps to decompose, permitting their stagnant waters to become fever breeders. Since he was not quite ready to give up his business, he wrote down precise instructions about what should be done at the bank and for him personally in case he fell ill a second time. It was well that he took this precaution: a second attack did come, leaving him helpless. Between spells of delirium, he was vaguely aware that his clerks were carrying out orders. They wrapped him in blankets and put him in the care of a servant. He was taken by fast river steamer and stagecoach to the more healthful climate of the Santa Clara Valley. Later, he could remember absolutely nothing about the trip.

There was no denying the fact that someone would have to bury him alongside Louis if he stayed much longer in Sacramento. In addition to the weakness left by the fever, he had a badly infected leg that refused to heal, and this made him hobble about in a turmoil of impatience and pain. Doctors advised him to rest the leg, so he rode horseback. Being sick was irksome. He cursed the interruption. For the first time in his career—this was far more serious than his early illness—he had to come to grips with the fact that to recover his health he must take leave of a land and a business that were prospering, but at the same time draining him of strength and health.

Finally he gave over the bank to the House of Rothschild. The ship on which he booked passage from California passed through the Golden Gate on April 8, 1852.

Had the trip been worth his while? Sailing south along the coast, he considered the question. Emphatically yes, he decided. True, as he went over his accounts he found that his clerks had pilfered a little, and he was annoyed not to have caught them doing it. But he was taking back to Russia twice the wealth he had when he left.

However, he was far from well. The Isthmus crossing lay ahead, an ordeal for a man in perfect health.

An ordeal it was. The leg wound worsened. There were drenching tropical rains. Food ran out. In company with other travelers who were crossing the mountain gorges and swamps sometimes by muleback and sometimes by dugout, he was obliged once to make a meal of "an immense lizzard, which we ate raw with the same voracious appetite as if it had been a roasted turkey." He would remember the miseries of the trip with horror. Not until May was he again at sea, safely en route to England.

Once more he put his faith in the sea, that old friend, old enemy whose behavior could never be guessed. When

he was nineteen and a homeless wanderer, it had be-
friended him, though it acted in the guise of enemy. He
was a bit superstitious about the sea. He tried to rest—always a hard task for Heinrich—and the sea was friendly
to him this voyage. He was nearly well before he left
England to make the return journey to Russia.

And now he chose to go by way of Germany, for something in him was homesick to see Ankershagen again with
its reminders of his boyhood. *"When I come back I shall
be a success."* He recalled the promise he had made to himself on leaving Hamburg years before. He could go back.

A few old people in Ankershagen recognized him, but
they were few indeed. The years had worked changes in
everything. He lingered for an hour one afternoon in the
garden house of his father's home where as a child he had
read and daydreamed. He discovered his own initials cut
on a linden tree in the garden not far from the little
haunted lake they called The Silver Chalice. Every window of the old house had scratches and marks. In the
study where he and his father used to argue about Troy
another bold "H.S." was cut crudely into a pane of glass.

He had wanted to leave an enduring mark everywhere
when he was only seven or eight years old, and he told
himself that he still had not lost that desire. Yes, he was
that same child, he thought, running his fingertips over
the letters, only his purpose now was sharper-cut than the
letters on the glass. He would be known, and he would
link the word "Troy" with the letters "H.S." The time
was close at hand.

None of the family any longer lived in Ankershagen.
His father had died. He located two of his married sisters

in nearby towns and visited them briefly before going on to St. Petersburg.

Here he began to pay serious court to a young woman who had been coolly uninterested in him before he went to California. But he was ready to take a wife. After that would come his retirement from business and the campaign to discover Troy.

X

Two years ago Catherine had seemed to be a woman
with so many suitors and so little time for Heinrich that
he had written off his own cause as hopeless. But he had
returned from the gold fields of California with new self-
assurance, and his air of having traveled and achieved
much in the world made him an imposing figure in St.
Petersburg society.

With honesty he could promise Catherine anything her
heart desired, and Heinrich meant by "anything" servants,
an apartment that was the last word in elegance even for
elegant St. Petersburg, and a coach and team of striking
beauty. He had, it seemed, the golden touch of King
Midas. All his business ventures were crowned with success. He was thirty and it was time to marry. He was convinced that a Russian woman, gently reared and of good
family, would be a suitable wife for him. She would make
a gracious companion for the coming adventure, the
search for Troy, but he considered it best to tell her about
all that later on. He married Catherine Lyschin on an
October day in 1852.

Her former attitude should have warned him. Before

the year was out they were quarreling, usually about money.

"Catherine," he would say, "you spend far too much."

"But you can afford it, Heinrich! Heavens, before we were married you used to say—"

"Whatever I said did not mean we could be extravagant." Always frugal in little things but a lover of the grand gesture, he brooded over what seemed to him her silly ways of wasting money, while she accused him of being downright stingy. Volatile tempers flared in small, sharp explosions.

Catherine had a son, but his coming did little to unite them. They were not drawn closer or made more tolerant of one another. Each new situation seemed only to create new conflict. For example, there was the question of where little Sergius should be sent to school.

"The schools in Paris are far superior to ours in St. Petersburg," Heinrich insisted. "Its academies are world-famous."

"But who wants to live in Paris?" Catherine demanded. "All my friends are here. It's all right for a visit, but—"

"After all," he argued, "it means only a few years. We want the child to have the best instruction. You will enjoy Paris."

"No," she replied, with such finality that he was surprised. "No, Heinrich."

Or there was the issue of studying languages. All very fine that he spoke eight and understood more than that. "Everyone I know," Catherine said, perhaps with justice, "considers Russian the international language. You go ahead and learn all the foreign gibberish you like. But please don't ask me to be a schoolgirl again. I don't like to study and I'm not good at it."

And Heinrich, who was adding Swedish and Polish to his list, alternately lost his patience or tried to be conciliatory. How did she expect them to maintain their comfortable standard of living, he asked, unless he met the demands of his expanding business with travel and new languages? Why wouldn't she humor him by writing to him in German while he was away, or in French? He was a home-loving man, often lonely when he had to spend holidays and family anniversaries in hotel rooms. She hated to write at all. Composing a letter was drudgery.

But when he first talked with her about the lifelong dream and the plan to retire, he was shaken by her response.

"Oh, Heinrich, what a wild notion!" She interrupted him before he was half through telling her how long he had been looking forward to his retirement and the Trojan adventure. "Why do you kill yourself making money and then sit up nights figuring out ridiculous plans to throw it away looking for an old buried city?"

He tried again, more gently, striving not to sound quarrelsome. She commented, "I can't see the slightest sense in it, my dear."

Indeed she did not, and she would not. There it was. She was a woman of physical beauty and charm, but not for an instant could she share his passion for the Trojan campaign. He tried to help her understand, reading to her and talking, almost pleading, and he went over it all again and often.

"Heinrich, whoever would want to go traipsing around

in those hot, Godforsaken places you mention? Think of the dirt and the smells. And all those disagreeable foreigners! Why can't we settle down? Everyone in St. Petersburg knows us, and there are marvelous balls this winter that we can't afford to miss." She was so appealing. "Why can't we enjoy life while we're young? You're hardly ever at home as it is."

During these years his business career seemed to go all the more smoothly, and this had the prior claim on his time. His long trips gave Catherine added cause for complaint. When he convinced himself that it was not possible to win her to his point of view, he gave up trying. Still, they had two more children. His eagerness to have them educated abroad became stronger as the children grew. So did Catherine's opposition. They were her children, too.

It seemed to Heinrich that the fates had played a cruel joke on him. He was bitter and angry that now, when he was so close to retirement, his greatest ambition should be blocked by the one woman out of all the world he had expected to help him achieve it.

There was one black, unnerving day in 1854 when he was threatened with the loss of everything he owned. Heinrich was spending September in Amsterdam, attending public auction sales of indigo. Dutch newspapers announced the outbreak of war between Russia and two nations that for centuries had been historic rivals, France and England. The charges and countercharges volleying between them gave Heinrich a sudden frightening foreboding. War could ruin him. He hurried back to Russia, distressed by every rumor and report. England's first-line battleships were throwing a blockade around Russian ports, and St. Petersburg was among the first to feel British power. The city was bottled up tight. All cargoes bound for St. Petersburg were rerouted and sent to the city of Memel, on the Baltic Sea, or to Königsberg. From either of these centers they could be forwarded by rail. Heinrich's chief concern was for the safety of many hundreds of chests of indigo, which he had bought from Schröder and Company, his old employers. He had a huge investment in the indigo and other goods. His stake in their arrival at Memel was, he thought as he raced for that city to supervise their transfer to railroad cars, nothing less than his whole fortune.

For weeks he had heard nothing from Catherine, not a line. The war had disrupted communications with his home office, too, and he was distraught with nerves and anxiety as he signed the register of the Hôtel de Prusse in Königsberg on the evening of October third. There was no transportation to Memel until tomorrow morning, and that would have to be by mail coach.

He stared out of his hotel room window thinking about the news of rapid troop movements and the blockade. This international tragedy could beggar him. If it should, Troy would have to await discovery by another man, not by Schliemann. Everything he had worked for, planned for, built toward . . .

His eye fell on an old Latin inscription carved over an ornate gateway just outside his hotel window. He read it aloud to himself absently:

"*Vultus fortunae variatur imagine lunae,*
  Crescit decrescit, constans persistere nescit."

It was several minutes before his mind took in its meaning. All at once it sank into him like a lead weight dropped into a pool:

> "*The face of fortune changes as the phases of the moon;*
> *It waxes and it wanes, and knows not how to remain constant.*"

He was not a superstitious man, he told himself furiously. Why was he shaking as if with a chill? For how many years had fortune been smiling on him? Not since his apprenticeship days had he known anything but the bright face of good luck, and what man can expect to be lucky forever?

The words struck deep, and he had a premonition of disaster. All night he could not get their senseless beat out of his head. On his way to the mail coach and with every turn of its wheels as it pounded toward Memel, the refrain dinned through his brain: "It waxes and it wanes, it waxes and it wanes . . ." Was the dark face of disaster on the rise?

At the station outside Memel he heard terrible news. Yesterday the wharves and most of the city had burned to the ground. Every merchant who had goods stored in its warehouses yesterday was bankrupt today.

> "*It waxes and it wanes . . .*"

Memel was ashes. His two shiploads of goods represented the investment of all the money he had earned in a lifetime of rigorous work. These were ashes. The city was a graveyard, he thought, staring somberly around him.

79

Charred walls and snags of chimneys jutted up among the piles of rubble like so many tottering headstones. A dozen hulks were drifting near the half-burned piers. Ships tied alongside the city wharves had gone up in flames along with the rest. His own consignments must have arrived only a day or two ago. If fortune smiled on him now, it was a derisive and vengeful smile.

He found his agent, a man named Meyer, who had the job of receiving his cargoes and transferring them to freight cars for transshipment to St. Petersburg. Meyer had the air of a man walking in his sleep. His face was lined with strain.

"My goods?" Heinrich asked hoarsely. "The shipments from Schröder and Company? They arrived?"

"Mr. Schliemann, they arrived three days ago."

"And—?"

Meyer looked at him and turned away. They were standing on ground that still felt hot through the soles of their boots, and the air was tainted with the smell of burned-out ruins. The agent gestured toward the water-front, where patches of smoke still hung overhead. "They are buried somewhere out there," he said.

"Out there." Heinrich repeated the words after him. There, too, his hopes, his life. There lay everything for which he had studied, saved, planned since boyhood. Two shiploads of indigo and war materiel, including saltpeter, lead, and brimstone, and they would have been worth a king's ransom in Russia this very minute. His campaign for Troy lay buried under that stinking wreckage.

Heinrich gave a final despairing look. Every warehouse on the waterfront of Memel either was razed to its foundations or had collapsed and slid into the dirty harbor water of the Baltic.

"Out there," Heinrich repeated dully. Then he left. A mail coach would depart for St. Petersburg in an hour. There was nothing to keep him in this graveyard. He would go back to Catherine and the children.

What now? He was at the station. Tired, excited people milled around, chattering of the tragedy. Heinrich looked at his hands and saw that they were trembling. The idiotic refrain, "It waxes and it wanes . . ." was chasing through his brain again.

What could he find to say to Catherine? This reversal changed everything. His luck had played out, that was all. He looked at matters in their stark outline. He was as empty-handed as the boy who trudged most of the way to the city of Hamburg to find a job as a grocer's apprentice.

The coach was late. He found a bench and sat down, wishing that he had hot coffee to stop the shaking of his hands and warm him out of this deathly chill. He hardly heard the buzz of conversation around him, and he cast about for some thought, some idea, to steady himself. Surely all his years with Schröder and Company would count when it came to getting started again. Yes, Schröder would extend credit. He was no upstart youngster; Schröder knew him and would be liberal with credit. Give him time enough and he could earn back some of what had gone up in yesterday's holocaust. Give him time enough . . . let the fighting end soon enough . . .

"As if it wasn't enough to have a war on our hands!" A man in a rusty-black overcoat was talking more to himself than anyone else, but the words were almost an echo of his own thoughts, and Heinrich was startled into listening. "I know a dozen men this has ruined," the stranger went on. "If we had been bombarded by the entire British fleet, it couldn't have been worse."

Heinrich said simply, making a statement of fact, "I have lost everything, too."

The stranger turned to him. "You've got plenty of company," he said wryly. "Memel is a city of paupers." He shrugged. "And then—some men are fortune's fools. Listen to this. It's my job to tell ten different businessmen that this fire has cost them every ruble they owned." He shook his head and rubbed his hands together, blowing on them in the cold evening air. "And, as I say, some men are fortune's fools." Heinrich's thoughts retreated. The man was a babbler, a nobody, overcome with a sense of his own importance.

"This man Schliemann, for instance. What a piece of luck! The only man who has lost not one case of indigo and not one pound of—"

"*What did you say?*" Heinrich leaped to his feet and gripped the man's coat. "What are you saying?"

"I said—what's the matter with you?"

Heinrich shook him. "What about Schliemann?"

"Schliemann is the only merchant who lost nothing."

"Why do you say that, you fool?"

"Who are you? How dare you? Stop!"

"Go on, go on—about Schliemann. Quick!"

"Sir! Let go of my coat! Schliemann sent two shiploads of goods to Meyer and Company—"

"You busybody! How do you know this?"

"I'm no busybody. I'm Meyer's chief clerk. When the steamers came in, every last one of our warehouses was full to overflowing. We had to put up some temporary wooden barracks alongside our stone warehouses to take care of Schliemann's cargo."

"Yes, wooden barracks, and—and—?"

"And those flimsy barracks were not touched! The fire just seemed to—to walk around them!"

Heinrich heard himself laughing. A few people looked at him in astonishment. As if wound by springs and unable to stop chattering, the clerk went on.

"The fire broke out in Meyer's big stone warehouse. That's it, over there." He gestured toward the north. "Or where it used to be. The wind was awful. Our warehouse went up first. Nothing could hold it back. It spread from the waterfront to the city. Don't ask me how such things happen, but the shacks where we stowed Schliemann's goods are not even singed. Everything he shipped out of Amsterdam is worth three or four times what it was a week ago—" He broke off because Heinrich's laughter had the sound of hysteria.

"What's wrong with you?"

"Wrong with me?" Heinrich caught his breath. "What could be wrong? God in heaven, man! My name is Schliemann!"

XI

"So delighted was the good Odysseus that he kissed
the fruitful earth, rejoicing in his own land."
The meeting with Athena. *Odyssey*, XIII, 353-354

He dismissed his guide at the foot of the mountain. They
were standing in the strong sunlight of Ithaca, that famous
island which lies to the west of Greece.

"You can find your way all right, sir?"

"As if it were my homeland," Heinrich replied, taking
coins from his pocket to pay the lad.

"But the ruins can't be seen easily unless one knows
where to look."

"Not for anyone who has seen them as often as I, my
boy."

"But—excuse me—I thought you were here for the
first time?"

"Physically, my friend. In my heart, many times. Good
day to you, and thanks."

The puzzled native boy watched him go on alone. This
strange tourist carried a copy of the *Odyssey* and spoke
Greek as though he had lived here many years. That was
what made him strange: he had said while they walked together that he was of German birth, and this his first
visit to Ithaca. The boy traced out a pattern in the dust

with his bare toe, watching until the visitor reached a turn in the pathway and disappeared.

It took Heinrich better than an hour to reach the crest of Mount Aëtos. He was in no particular hurry. Before he was at the summit he halted, for his heart was racing, and not just from the climb. It may have been here, he thought, right *here*, that Odysseus' old dog banged his wispy tail on the earth when he recognized his long-absent master. Overhead the sky was such a blue that it recalled Homer's gracious adjective, *cerulean.* Tomorrow he would do a little experimental digging in this ground. The natives said that the summit was the place where Odysseus the seafarer had built his castle.

It was a hot summer day in 1868, so hot that only a tourist would step outside the shade of olive trees, if he must be out of doors at all. Heinrich noticed neither the heat, the dust, nor the wilted droop of his linen suit. He had begun his second life, the life of exploring and discovery.

The final plan of attack, he was thinking as he resumed his uphill walk, was still to be decided before he could settle down systematically to the work of excavating Troy. He was going to make this visit to Ithaca a casual one, then go on to the ruins of Mycenae, and finally to the Plain of Troy, in Asia Minor. Heinrich's career as businessman was behind him. The career of Schliemann the discoverer had begun. Against the background of Homer's wine-dark sea rose the gray-green slopes of Odysseus' homeland, and Heinrich Schliemann gazed at them with awe and joy in his heart.

This visit would have to be short, chiefly because he was

only testing his own thinking. Many of his theories were in sharp conflict with the opinions of other scholars. He could call them "other scholars," for he was beginning to claim some authority himself. With most of them he differed on two main points: the location of the royal tombs of Mycenae, and the exact location of the city of Troy.

The Mycenaean tombs were the burial vaults of Agamemnon and those men of his bodyguard who had been slain with him on their return from the Trojan War. Pausanias, the old Greek traveler and geographer whom some scholars regarded as a gossip, had written about what he saw in Mycenae during his own globe-trotting in the second century. He had left a rather ambiguous account of the location of the legendary tombs. Historical rumor trickling down the centuries said that fabulous treasure in gold and jewels was buried with the murdered king and his henchmen. During Heinrich's lifetime a couple of expeditions had failed to find the burial ground. He was convinced that he knew the reason for their failure: the expedition leaders had misinterpreted the words of Pausanias. *Dummköpfe!*

Heinrich's second theory of course concerned Troy. The archeologists of his day who conceded that there may have been such a city located it near a village called Bounarbashi, on the Plain of Troy. He would go and see for himself, but he was skeptical in advance; he had other ideas, based on intensive studies he had just completed. He was going to take Pausanias's own guidebook to Mycenae, and he would take Homer's poems to Troy, and there map out his strategy on the spot, under the guidance of the ancient authorities. How stupid it was, he thought, to quarrel over trifles! The early writers had made statements that could serve as valuable clues if one had the wit and the insight to interpret them properly.

With an abrupt twist of the pathway he found himself on the mountaintop. Beyond lay the Ionian Sea, dappled with noon sunlight. He had climbed above the rugged foothills. Somewhere on this height lay the palace ruins.

Heinrich sat down and wiped the sweat from his face with a handkerchief. Ah! This was better! He stretched out in a shady spot and rested his eyes on the sea, wondering how many times in fantasies he had seen himself exactly where he was, doing exactly what he was doing now. To be sure, it was not Troy; but the earth beneath him was Ithaca, and on it Odysseus had walked. He put out his hand and touched the earth. It was a reverent act.

While his eyes scanned the horizon, he knew once more the feeling of triumph he had had when he read the *Iliad* and the *Odyssey* in Greek for the first time. Never would he forget the expression on his teacher's face when he began to read Greek, the language he had forbidden himself to learn until he was ready for retirement. Heinrich had begun to study Greek on the very day he learned that the Crimean War was over.

The memory of Theokletos Vimpos, his teacher, made him smile. His face had a look of dismay, almost of alarm, the first time Heinrich lifted his voice in a joyous shout to read a passage in Homer that he knew in German translation.

For two years Heinrich read Homer and other Greek writers as no schoolboy ever did; he read avidly, tramping about and roaring in his excitement. Vimpos, an Orthodox

Greek priest, got used to the German and his volcanic way of studying. Different as the two men were in personality, they had become strong friends, sharing a love for Homer and a respect for one another that Heinrich knew would last their lifetimes. The thought of his dear friend Vimpos made him wish he were sitting here beside him.

Sometimes during the days of the Crimean War, Heinrich reflected, it might appear that the boy who dreamed of finding the rutted streets and windy towers of Troy had been lost in the man who traded in the goods of war. California, the destroyer of so many men's hopes, and Memel, where fortunes were wiped out by flames and the war that brought distress to thousands—each of these had only sped him on his way faster, and each had made him richer.

"I don't deny that I love money," he had defended himself to Catherine during one of the perpetual arguments. "But I love it only as the means of realizing the great idea of my life."

When he had first made arrangements for his retirement in 1858, he had as much money as he wanted or might need. Withdrawing from all his business interests seemed then to be both safe and possible.

Again the unexpected, the unforeseen. The change in his plan was forced by business conditions, but Catherine's actions had been upsetting, too. He had suggested that she join him in a leisurely trip abroad that spring. On their return he would liquidate his business. Catherine flatly refused to go with him. So he went alone to some of the countries he had never seen, visiting Sweden, Denmark, and Italy. Then to Egypt, where his first glimpse of the pyramids was from a sailboat on the Nile. Here he learned Arabic. In the summer of 1859, still alone, he had reached Athens, the home of Pericles, Socrates, and Plato, a city second only to Troy itself in the chronicles of the Western world.

Heinrich rose. The sun was less blinding now. He picked his way among rocks and thorny underbrush to some scattered but clearly visible ruins of a wall running as far across the mountaintop as his eye could see. He traced them out on foot and examined the masonry. The gnarled roots of a very old and still vital olive tree stood among the ruins, and he ran his fingertips along the trunk. Could it be, he mused? Was it conceivable that this was the very tree from whose living limbs Odysseus had carved his bed? Were these really the ruins of the castle where the long-suffering Penelope awaited her husband's return?

He sat down by the tree and opened his little Greek book to reread the story of Odysseus' homecoming—it might have been to this mountain. He lost himself in the poem, and when he finally looked up from the book, his mind went back to his own wanderings.

He had returned from his travels to find, in 1859, that retirement was no easy matter of closing his desk and locking the office door; there were too many desks and too many doors to his far-flung business interests, and unstable conditions both in Russia and foreign lands did not permit him to withdraw. But by 1863 he accomplished it, and he put commerce behind him for scholarship.

He sailed for Tunis in April of 1864 to walk among the remains of Carthage. He was for the first time a man unfettered and moving toward his destiny. There were ports of call in the modern world that sparked his curiosity. The fragments and shards of half-forgotten cities were very inviting, but first he wanted to know the modern world as well as he would acquaint himself with the ancient. This was the period when he wished to wander about in the nooks and crannies of the world, so he sailed around it—alone, as usual—stopping where he pleased as his fancy directed: India and the Himalayas, China and her Great Wall. There was nothing anywhere on the face of the whole spinning planet that failed to draw his attention. Japan, and America again; Mexico, and so back to Paris, where he made one more urgent appeal, imploring Catherine to join him.

It was then 1866. Again she refused to come. This seemed to Heinrich the ultimate proof that their marriage was ended. They had been long estranged, and although then, as always, he found failures hard to accept, having known so few, he had to acknowledge that this was a major one.

Now evening was coming on. He returned to the footpath and began the downhill walk. Here he was in Ithaca, he thought. Alone. All events and all his plans had been in preparation for this day and the ones soon to come. For the last two years he had lived in Paris studying history and archeology to inform his mind for the herculean task of excavating Troy. He belonged to many learned scientific and historical societies. He was author of the book *China and Japan*, which grew out of his first travels to the Orient.

A few goats that had straggled from a flock were grazing beside the path. Their herdsman was eating his evening meal beneath a tree. Heinrich lifted his cane in salute and the peasant waved back to him.

All told, it was six hundred feet from the top of Mount Aëtos to sea level. Where the path leveled off, the native boy who had been his guide came running eagerly toward him.

"Sir, are you going to the castle again tomorrow? May I take you?"

Heinrich considered. He intended to take a load of tools to the ruins for a trial digging. Well, the lad could help.

"Yes, tomorrow you may join me. We shall have some things to carry."

"Tomorrow, sir! I shall be waiting for you in the village."

He would not stay long, Heinrich reflected; he must be getting along to Mycenae, and then to the Trojan Plain. Even so, he could stay there only long enough to test his theory about where the city of Troy had stood.

This was the year that had to bring an end to his one still-pressing problem, the divorce. Until that was done he could not be at peace with himself.

A cool sea wind was stirring the leaves of the olive trees. He was, he told himself, a distinguished man. He was in Ithaca. This was a homecoming, too. But he was lonely. For him there was no Penelope.

XII

"For he truly thought he would take Priam's city that
very day . . ."

Agamemnon's dream. Iliad, II, 37

Troy!

He squinted his eyes and shaded them with his hand. Try
as he would, he could not really see the coast, and there
was nothing wrong with his vision.

Something—not his eyesight!—was wrong.

He must not feel so jubilant, he cautioned himself, not
this soon. Nothing was proved. Still . . . he flicked his
walking stick at the grasses about him and twirled it in the
air in his excitement. This morning at dawn he had started
walking. He had commenced at the shore of the Hellespont and marched purposefully across the plain until he
began to scale this steep, rocky rise. Now he was just behind the Turkish village of Bounarbashi, standing on the
hill that those few scholars who believed in a historic
Troy thought to be its likeliest site.

Troy, here?

Something was wrong!

In the *Iliad* Homer says that the Greek soldiers made
the round trip from their hollow ships, beached on the
shore, to the fortress-city and back again several times a
day. But to get from the Hellespont to this hill behind the

town Heinrich had done nearly four hours of hard walk-ing, and he had not dillydallied along the way. To start from the coast and get here, then complete the return journey, would take a man most of the hours of daylight.

Something was wrong!

He pulled his *Iliad* from his pocket and opened it to Book XI, finding the passage in which Homer talks about a day of very heavy battle. Heinrich reviewed that day's happenings:

In the morning the hard-fighting Greeks drive the Tro-jans to the Scaean Gate. They are themselves pushed back to their many-oared ships, where horrible slaughter takes place. This is the same day that Patroclus tries three different times to scale the walls of Troy. The Trojans have now been beaten back to their own battlements. The struggle continues near the Scaean Gate until nightfall. *It is all one battle and it all occurs in the course of one day.* Yet in this short time the Greeks, whether advancing or retreating, have three times covered the miles separating the city and the shore.

Heinrich spun around and started walking to the south-east. Where was Mount Ida, "rich in springs"? It should be visible through its crown of rising and falling clouds to the south. But from this vantage point Mount Ida could not be seen at all!

Heinrich gazed north to the Hellespont. The strip of blue water was very hard to discern. Yet the Trojans al-ways saw it clearly from their windy towers, just as they could see Mount Ida at the southern end of the plain.

Something was wrong. Several things were wrong!

A small river flowed lazily on the plain below. Certain

scholars declared that the insignificant little brook was the mighty Scamander. This, the Scamander? Either Homer was guilty of wild exaggeration, or his present-day readers were reckless with observable fact. To grant Bounarbashi the honor of being Troy, one must do some rewriting of Book XVI of the *Iliad*, because in it Homer said that the Scamander flowed between the city of Troy and the Greek ships, while this meager stream Heinrich was staring at lay on the wrong side of the hill entirely!

Heinrich went on arguing with himself while he tapped his walking stick smartly against his boot: how could Achilles pursue Hector three times—*three* times, mind you!—around the walls of a city built on such cliffs as these? They jutted up too sharply from the floor of the plain. The surface of the hill was so limited in area that not by the tightest stretch of imagination could one visualize lofty temples, palaces, and courtyards on its rugged, uneven top.

But there were more tests to apply. If Homer said that a certain action was performed by human heroes, then it had to be humanly possible. Of nothing was Heinrich more profoundly sure. The two heroes of the *Iliad* would have had to go down the south side of the cliffs to make a circuit of the city. Heinrich strode over to the south side and began to run, a strange figure on a strange errand, but if anyone besides a few browsing sheep saw him, he did not know or care.

And here the cliffs sheared off at an angle of forty-five degrees. He was panting for breath and could not go another step forward. Indeed, he had to get on all fours and crawl down backward.

It took fifteen minutes to scramble and slide down to the plain. He arrived winded and with the knee of one trouser leg in tatters. Only goats could make such a descent! While he recovered his breath, Heinrich opened his *Iliad* to Book XXII and read again how Hector tries to elude his enemy by slipping close to the high walls, so that the arrows of his own men in the battlements above may pass over him harmlessly and rain down on Achilles. But time and again Achilles cuts him off and forces him away from the walls and out upon the open plain.

Nobody, Heinrich thought happily, had pursued any-body around any walls on the hill of Bounarbashi!

If they had tried that famous chase here, *both* Achilles and Hector would have died—of broken necks!

He was hungry, but too elated to think about food. He sprinted over to the spot near the hill where innumerable living springs flowed from the ground. To many scholars these springs were the clinching argument that supported their Bounarbashi-Troy theory. He spent the afternoon tracing them out and counting them. Homer mentions two springs near Troy, one of cold water, one of warm. And, Heinrich reminded himself for the hundredth time, Homer was seldom careless in details. If he said that the Greek foot soldiers covered the ground between sea and city *several* times between morning and night, Troy could not lie *eight* miles inland, but at the most no more than three. If Homer said that *two* springs gushed from the earth then two it was, and not—as he had just counted—*thirty-four!*

Heinrich's mood changed from intense studious concen-tration to amused gaiety. Something was wrong, decidedly, wonderfully wrong, with that old theory! *Dummköpfe!*

And he took off lightheartedly for the home of his new friend, Frank Calvert, who had invited him to spend the evening.

Calvert was the exceptionally able diplomat who was serving as the American vice-consul to the Dardanelles. He had done some thinking, himself, about the enigma of Troy, because he was an enthusiastic student of archeology, and he had been mulling over the problem of the Troad, as the region of Troy was called. The friendship of these two men was based on a wealth of mutual interests in history and science and the romance of the Trojan legends.

"I can't say I fully agree with you, Schliemann," Calvert commented a few days later. They were back on the site where, near Bounarbashi, a gang of native workmen hired by Heinrich was beginning to sink the first shafts for some exploratory digging. "I'm not convinced that you will prove one theory merely by disproving another." The two men had passed many hours amiably arguing every aspect of the possibility that Bounarbashi was Troy. "Of course," Calvert continued, "I'm not at all satisfied that it qualifies as the site, and I haven't been for years. But the leading scholars I've read do seem to be in general agreement. And one has to admit that local tradition is a powerful argument."

"Scholarship!" Heinrich scoffed. "Tradition! Fiddlesticks! Has no one really read Homer?"

Calvert agreed that if Heinrich were to rule out Bounarbashi, then Strabo's description of a city called Novum Ilium deserved study. Strabo, the Greek geographer, had been a contemporary of Jesus. His writings frequently

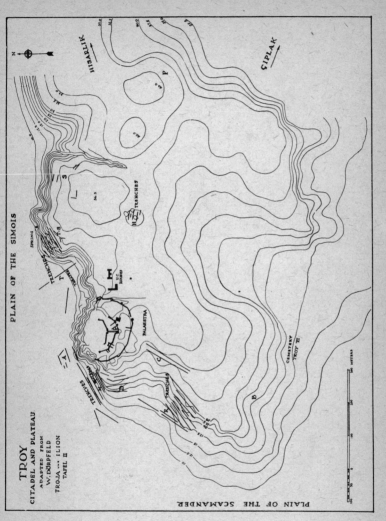

Plan of Trojan Citadel and Plateau. *(From Troy, vol. III, by Blegen, Caskey, Rawson, and Sperling, Princeton University Press, 1953)*

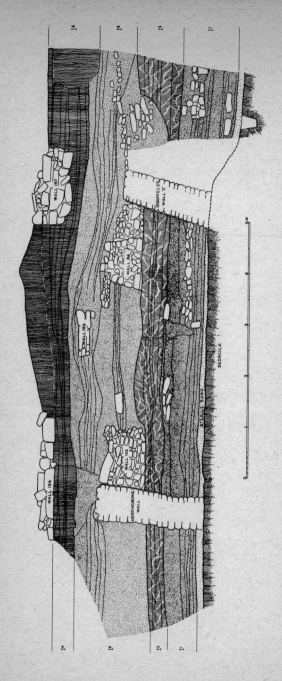

Diagrammatic section of strata visible in west bank of Schliemann's Great Trench. (*From* Troy, *vol. I, by Blegen et al., Princeton University Press, 1950*)

mention a city known as Novum Ilium, or New Troy. As to its exact location neither archeologists nor natives had the slightest quarrel. It was a hilly region just three miles from the Hellespont.

"If your men find nothing conclusive on Bounarbashi, what then?" Calvert's expression hinted that he could guess the answer, but so far, Heinrich had not announced his plans.

"Then," replied Heinrich, "we shall put down some shafts at Novum Ilium." His eyes were dancing.

Calvert laughed. "Of course!"

The workmen dug pits in hundreds of assigned places between the springs and the topmost reach of the cliffs behind Bounarbashi village. Each time, they struck bedrock at very slight depth. They brought up not one fragment of pottery, no implements, nothing of ancient human fabrication, except at the south end; but Calvert and Heinrich agreed that the ruins uncovered here had belonged not to Troy but to an ancient city clearly identified as Gergis. To Heinrich it was a most satisfying failure, since it convinced him once and for all that Bounarbashi never could have been Troy.

Later that month he went alone to pace out the miles that lay between the sea and another plateau. This region was in the northwest section of the plain and it was still referred to as New Troy. Here stood a ridge of long barren hills. The spur was a plateau, a naturally fortified rise of the land. On one end of this plateau stood the modern Turkish village called Hissarlik, the name itself meaning "place of fortresses." The plateau lifted in an easy, gentle slope from the village to reach a height of 160 feet above the floor of the plain. A few wind-riven oaks and random grasses clung to life on its flat, desolate top.

To Heinrich Schliemann, by all the logic of common sense, Homer, and human history, this escarpment—called Hissarlik because of the village on one of its shoulders—was the only place where a key stronghold like the citadel of Troy could have stood. On this site a city would have been doubly protected: by man-made walls and by the gradualness of the elevation that gave it dominion over the plain. The hillsides were steep, but they were not precipitous. And the Hellespont was three miles away. Thus a city occupying these heights could stand off attacks from predatory armies and demand toll of ships approaching the Dardanelles. On the other hand, he reminded himself, Bounarbashi lay *eight* miles in a straight line due south of the Hellespont!

Heinrich's measured walk had taken a few minutes less than two hours. He was climbing the hill of Hissarlik quite effortlessly. And now he felt his heart begin to pound. When he gazed down across the distance he had just traveled, his mind's eye peopled the plain below with armies. From the top of Hissarlik the sea was brilliantly clear! He wanted to shout. But he stood utterly silent and reined in his enthusiasm, telling himself firmly that only one test had been met. No, two: Achilles and Hector could most certainly have slipped along the sides of walls on this hill. But there were other tests to be met before he could be positive. He would see Calvert.

"Hissarlik is very promising," he told Frank. "But where are the springs? I could see none. If every other qualification were met, I still would have to be dubious until I found the springs."

Sometimes Calvert accompanied him on these walking trips. He was a stimulating companion, and he was eager to have Heinrich start a campaign of exploration here. In fact, he had become ardently convinced that Hissarlik was the site of Troy even before Heinrich would commit himself. As luck had it, Calvert himself owned more than half the mound of Hissarlik. He had even probed into the hillside here and there some years previously and had brought up pieces of a very ancient wall. Until Heinrich's coming he had attached no great importance to them.

But for Heinrich each piece of the puzzle must fit every other; the springs, the river, and the sea—each must fall into its proper place and join precisely. "To be sure," he would muse, "springs disappear and rivers are forever altering their courses."

"And the coast line washes away imperceptibly year after year," Calvert would agree.

"Or else it is building up," Heinrich added, "growing larger by the addition of alluvial soil. Even so, even so, I must find the springs and the river that Homer says were just outside the city."

He was gone once for several days. On his return he was in a glow of high spirits. "How blind I have been! Come with me, Calvert. I must have crossed and recrossed it a dozen times and not seen it for what it is."

He had discovered a dry river bed, so transformed by erosion that without careful study one could not perceive what its original course had been.

Soon Heinrich disappeared again for a whole day, to come back with news of finding a second ancient river bed, one that met the first.

"Here is the junction," he exulted. "This is where, ages ago, the Scamander and the Simois joined, exactly as Homer said."

"And the springs?" Calvert asked. He had to conceal his amusement over his friend's sudden crestfallen air.

"Ach!" said Heinrich. "Those springs! Those miserable springs!"

But he kept searching. And he found them. There were two, one four hundred yards, another a thousand yards, from Hissarlik. They had escaped his notice because they were still in use by the natives, who had built heavy stone enclosures about them and drained off their waters into cattle troughs.

The more Heinrich talked and thumped the pages of his Homer, the more fervently Calvert agreed with him. "Why do you hold back?" he finally asked. "You've made your point, Schliemann. Why don't you start excavating at once? Tomorrow!"

There was nothing that Heinrich wanted more. But the divorce must be settled. This trip to the Troad had been, anyway, a preliminary survey, made for a purpose it had served well: to show that his theories held up under crucial testing. The same had been true at Mycenae. There he had seen the ruins of walls so old that the natives declared their huge rough-hewn blocks had been set in place by one-eyed giants, the Cyclopes of mythology. He was certain that he knew precisely where to go to unearth the tombs of Agamemnon and his soldiers.

"No," he told Calvert ruefully. "Not tomorrow. And not this year." They were at the base of the plateau called Hissarlik, standing in the rubble of the dry river bed. Calvert studied his friend's face and tactfully asked no further questions. He said only, "But of course you will come back to Troy."

Heinrich leaned thoughtfully on his walking stick and stared upward, frowning at the vast dark mass of Hissarlik. What did it hide? Would his stubborn belief be vindicated? A year from now, perhaps, would these hands of his hold treasure and gold taken from hiding places deep within this hill? Or—he let the idea take shape—would its depths be as barren as its empty surface? Then laughter would be ringing around the world at the name of Heinrich Schliemann.

No! He permitted the ugly thought of failure to take form only this one time, and he never allowed it to return. *This was Troy*. In this immense mound were lost chapters from the pages of man's history on the wrinkled earth. Somewhere amid these layers of soil must be armor and jewels and gold buried along with the foundation stones of tall towers and graceful temples. He believed that. And he would find them. He would prove that Troy had existed, the Troy seen by Homer who had sung of it and created it eternal.

Of course, there might be other rewards in addition to the fame of being its discoverer. If the gold he found should make him a richer man than he already was, that, too, would be good! It was in the laps of the gods as to whether he found golden treasure and his name became illustrious. But hunt for Troy he must. He had to. It was his destiny.

So he barricaded himself against doubt and bolted the gates of his mind against the fear of failure.

"I shall not rest until I am free to return," he said.

Calvert nodded. "I understand. May it be soon."

XIII

"You surpass all women in beauty, stature, and wisdom."
Eurymachus to Penelope. *Odyssey*, XVIII, 248-249

He turned the photograph this way and that and held it to the light. He put it down and walked away, but he always came back to it. Though there were other photographs on his desk, he came back each time to this one. Smoldering eyes were deep set in the well-formed face. The hair must be auburn, he judged, looking at it intently. But the eyes . . . the eyes held him. There was a purity about them, a radiance.

"My main requirement is a good and loving heart," Heinrich had written his dear friend Theokletos Vimpos. Since they had seen each other last, Vimpos had been named Archbishop of Greece. In his letter Heinrich had followed the Old World way of doing things. He had asked his friend and teacher to send him pictures of several of the most promising, most suitable young women of Athens, from among whom he would choose one to marry.

He was then living in Indianapolis until his divorce from Catherine should be granted. Divorce laws in the United States were more liberal than in Russia, so this was his temporary home. He had established his American citizenship.

Vimpos had sent him photographs. The one which captured Heinrich's heart was of Sophia Engastromenos. She was just seventeen, and it happened, too, that she was a cousin of Vimpos and was planning to become a teacher. Vimpos wrote that she knew Homer and was well read in classical Greek. Heinrich had made a good education one of his requirements, although the main one was that "good and loving heart."

And in the spring of 1869 he wrote Vimpos that he would arrive in Athens the following August to meet Sophia, or Sophie, as he already preferred to call her. When the matter was reduced to simplest terms, Heinrich felt that what he needed most to companion him in the Trojan adventure was a wife who would share his passion for the noble past. He could have had his choice of beautiful and eligible women in half a dozen countries, but the lesson in disillusion that he had learned from Catherine had taught him what he valued most highly in a wife.

While he waited for the separation from Catherine to become legal, he completed his book *Ithaca, the Peloponnesus, and Troy.* A copy of it went to the University of Rostock. His friend Carl Andres, that same man who had taught him Latin thirty-seven years ago in Kalkhorst, had helped him prepare the story of his career. It was written in classical Greek and published with the book. The university granted Heinrich a doctorate in philosophy for this publication.

The pastor's son and grocer's apprentice, the absent-minded errand boy of Amsterdam had come a very long way. He was today Doctor Schliemann: archeologist, author, doctor of philosophy. And he was supremely confident in his own mind that he had found the site of historical Troy.

When the divorce was made final, he sailed immediately for Athens. The archbishop made the introductions to Sophia's family, who wined and dined Heinrich for several days. The neighbors chattered about this wealthy German from Russia and America who was here in Greece to marry one of their own girls. It might all be a trifle hard to explain, but what a catch he was! What a lucky girl, Sophia!

The first time Heinrich and Sophie could manage to be alone, they went walking together. Away from the curious eyes of her relatives and the stares of the friendly, talkative neighbors, he put a few questions to her. "Would you like to go on a long journey?" he asked.

She was modest and unsure of herself. The great eyes that had won him in her photograph were hesitant to meet his. She longed to make a good impression.

"Ah, yes," she said softly.

"What passages in Homer do you know by heart?" And he was delighted as she began to recite verse after verse, though in such a subdued voice that he had to say, "Excellent, but speak up, speak up!"

It was a courtship not like any he had ever heard of, or she, either; yet it was a courtship. Sophie tried to keep up with his long strides, and she went on reciting Homer as he asked, but a little breathlessly because he walked so fast.

When they returned to her parents' house, he was still asking questions. He thought he saw eyes peering at them from the windows, but he chose to ignore them. "Sophie, tell me: why do you wish to marry me?" he asked.

Her eyes were somber and her young face very thought-ful. She said distinctly, looking at him, "Because my parents have told me that you are a rich man."

Heinrich was thunderstruck. His face clouded. She couldn't understand why, for she had answered him with absolute candor, just as her cousin the archbishop had advised her to do. ("No lies, Sophie. Answer truthfully anything you may be asked.")

Heinrich muttered something, turned away, and disappeared down the street. Her parents rushed out. She told them what had happened. Vimpos heard her story and shook his head.

"Did I do wrong?" she asked, very troubled.

"No, my child, no. Perhaps," said the archbishop, "he is not accustomed to hearing the truth in such forthright words."

Vimpos knew that Heinrich was drawing the worst possible conclusion from her innocent reply. Probably her parents had told her this along with many other things, and her clear-eyed simplicity reflected their motives, but not her own. Vimpos went to find Heinrich at his hotel and they talked half the night. Heinrich could not deny that he was already half in love with her. And, as Vimpos said, it was folly to assume that her parents could afford to be indifferent to his obvious wealth and station in life. But as to the girl—!

No one but his dear friend Vimpos could have reassured him enough to make him see that her very directness was the proof of her sincerity. Sophie was no fortune hunter; far from it. Her words were all the evidence he needed to show what an obedient daughter she was and how devastatingly truthful a woman! When he saw her again, he read her affection for him in her lustrous eyes. He had found his good and loving heart.

Until they were married they spoke together only in Greek. Afterward he began to teach her German, and she learned gladly, pleased by his pride in her progress. He had plans for her to learn French, of course, and then English, and perhaps Russian. He told her that when they were on the mound of Hissarlik, he at work on the soil of Troy, she would read aloud to him from the *Iliad* and he would feel blessed by the immortal gods.

There were museums he wanted to show her, books on history and archeology for her to read so that she could understand his work and his discussions.

Whether he was more in love with the promises life held or with his beautiful Sophie of the dark, adoring eyes, it was hard to say. But Heinrich was deeply in love. His wife was his companion, eager to learn and share and be with him, whatever he proposed. He had never known happiness like this, nor anything like her love.

He took Sophie to the Plain of Troy in April, 1870. Life's greatest adventure had begun for him and his wife.

XIV

"This expedition of yours will not be useless, nor will
it end in failure."
          Athena to Telemachus. *Odyssey*, II, 273

Over the tip of the island of Samothrace far out at sea
the clouds were gathering. Homer had described their dark
masses exactly as they looked to Heinrich's eyes. Samothrace was the throne of Poseidon, the sea god, who was
second in power over mankind to Olympian Zeus himself.
The clouds might portend a storm bearing down from the
northwest. But clouds were shaping over snow-capped
Mount Ida, too. Lightning was shimmering in the southeast
over its snowy summit. Would Zeus the Thunderer speak
tonight, or was the wind from the sea god's domain?

Under the incredible blue of the Trojan sky Heinrich
was showing his wife what any Trojan could have seen
from this hilltop thousands of years ago. She was beside
him, attentive and still. Greece was her birthplace and
Germany his, but it was he who knew intimately every jut-
ting arm of the sea and the name of each of the islands that
formed part of her heritage. She was his pupil in all things.

"Tenedos is over there," Heinrich said, using his walking
stick to direct her eyes southward and to the west. "When
the Greeks finished building their wooden horse and had
the trap all set for the Trojans, they withdrew their fleet to

that island. See how near it is! You can almost reach out and put it in your hand! They hid behind its crags until the trap was sprung and then rushed back to burn the city."

He felt very young, very fortunate, and his heart was full. He took Sophie's hand. "I think they are watching us," he said.

"Who, Heinrich? Who watches us?"

"Zeus and Poseidon," he said. "They must know that we are going to begin work on the hill tomorrow."

"And you think they will be angry?"

"I don't know. We shall have to disturb the bones of many Trojans. This is sacred soil."

Sophie said, as serious as he, "But they will surely understand. You will restore Troy to her place in the sun. And the gods who watched over Ilios—Mars and Venus—they will favor us, Heinrich."

It was October, very late in the year—and this was 1871 —to begin digging, but the air was winy, and there had been too many annoying delays already, a result of the need to get legal permission from the Turkish government to work this section of Hissarlik that Calvert did not own. Neither was Heinrich at all pleased about having to live a mile and a quarter away from the site of the campaign, in the village of Chiblak. The wheelbarrows and digging tools he was able to buy were not of the finest quality, and he would have liked to double the number of men in this first work gang.

But when he spoke of these things with irritation to Sophie, she would remind him that it was merely the beginning. Conditions were not ideal, perhaps, but think! *They were at Troy!* And his face would gradually soften and he would cease knocking his walking stick against his dusty boot to return her smile, shrug, and go briskly off to supervise the eighty natives who had begun burrowing into the earth.

All that month Heinrich had them sink shafts and make soil tests. They began a large trench on the face of the steep northern slope. By barrowloads and bucketfuls the earth of ages was loosened; Heinrich ran his fingers through it a hundred times an hour as layer upon layer was scooped up and removed. Down went the trench, sometimes a foot a day, sometimes only an inch or two. Fragments of pottery began to turn up under the workmen's picks. Studying them, Heinrich declared that they were very old—older than Roman, but not to be called Greek. He was too impatient to stop when they encountered the foundation stones of a building that seemed to run about sixty feet in length. From inscriptions on several of its large, hand-wrought stones, he decided quickly that it was a Hellenic ruin, and he gave orders to slash down through it. He was seeking the remains of Troy, far, far older than these stones. Other archeologists might have rhapsodized over things such as these, but not Heinrich. *Dig deeper*, he ordered. *Move along. We waste time.* And the walking stick beat against his boot.

By the first of November the north wind was pitiless. The men complained and many quit. He raised wages and urged the gang on, but they grumbled. It exasperated him that they did not share his eagerness.

Beneath the Hellenic remains they struck more stones and some coarse pottery, obviously made by hand. He hesitated to give it a name. In point of fact, he knew nothing to compare it with. It was very rudely made stuff. He was on fire with curiosity and impatience. Winter was almost here, and nothing had been found that clearly and unmistakably could be called of Trojan origin.

In the layer of soil beneath the pottery fragments were house walls made of stone. Among the remains of these walls lay curious implements, including stone grinders and more of the strange coarse pottery. Sun-dried bricks began to appear. At thirty feet below the surface were many large hand-hewn blocks. As the crusted earth was pried and dusted away from them, it seemed to Heinrich that the stones of these house walls must have been shaken violently apart, possibly by an earthquake.

By now Heinrich was sorely puzzled. There was no disputing that these implements, this pottery, and the old house walls were of great age, but they were primitive and crude. The Trojans of Homer's poems were a civilized people possessed of rare skills and arts. These articles were about as clumsy as those of Stone Age man.

By late November the exposed plateau was too cold and the wind too fierce to permit the work to continue. Heinrich dismissed his natives and went with Sophie to Paris, where they made their permanent home. The winter months seemed to drag, although he devoted them to planning a more thorough campaign. It would be far better equipped and staffed than last year's. Orders went out to Schröder and Company for the best British-made wheelbarrows, spades, and pickaxes. An engineer was engaged to make maps and plans. Heinrich was reaching full stride.

By March he and Sophie were back on the site. Now three overseers bossed one hundred and thirty workmen.

Heinrich had learned Turkish as a matter of course so as to write and speak the language of the people in whose land he worked.

He pushed ahead with a plan that was a daring and gigantic engineering project in itself. The science of archeology was in its infancy. Men engaged in excavating had few precedents to guide them. Heinrich was spurred along as he had been at the age of eight by the belief that Troy did exist and that proof of its existence could be found by a persistent excavator. He was bound to find it, he thought, if only he could dig deep enough. The remains of late Greek life and Roman occupation in this locale did not concern him. He was searching for Homer's Troy.

His project consisted of cutting a vast trench through the north end of the hill of Hissarlik. He would lay open the hillside with a great slash that would expose a cross-section and show its layers as clearly as a drawn diagram. It was bold. It was a giant's labor. In terms of man-hours and wheelbarrow loads of earth to be carried off and dumped, it would require months of toil by men and draft animals. He would slice down twenty, thirty, forty feet in depth, and bring to view each successive stratum, or layer, of soil. The fact was already clear to Heinrich that this hilltop had been occupied by humans for dozens of centuries. One settlement must have been built helter-skelter upon another. There must have been not one city of Troy, but several, perhaps five or six, and maybe as many as seven, built one atop the other. A great gash cut through the hill would disclose, he thought, exactly how they lay in relation to one another, these lost and buried cities, and then he could study each separately. His intent was to dig straight down to virgin soil. If he could find ruins resting on what had been the original earth of the hill, then, he reasoned, he would be touching the original Troy.

Carpenters were busy all during April of 1872 constructing a three-room house on the hilltop for the Schliemanns. Heinrich could now be close to the trenches all the time, and Sophie had a kitchen where she could cook the sort of food he liked. When she was not at his side, Sophie was off to some other part of Hissarlik, watching the progress of the digging. Heinrich was surprised at how readily she grasped the problems that came up. She always shared his relief when they worked out solutions. And she seemed to have a man's endurance, his Sophie, not even complaining once about being away from the child who had been born to them in France last winter. They had named their daughter Andromache. She stayed in a nurse's care in Paris; conditions here on Hissarlik were too trying for an infant. Often while Heinrich supervised his gangs, Sophie would sit in the brilliant sun beside him, reading his favorite passages from the *Iliad*—reading beautifully in her clear, calm voice, so that he had the words he loved most in the world to accompany the work he most wanted to do.

The great trench began to take form. It ran more than two hundred feet in width, and no one ventured to guess how far down it would sink. What lay within? The question was always in the air, spoken or unspoken.

Spring became summer, an early summer in this part of the world. Winds whipped off the Aegean to spin the dust of the topsoil around the diggers. Their nostrils stung and their eyes hurt. Few of the workmen owned goggles.

They muffled their faces with scarves to shut out the dust, but it made them suffer cruelly. On an especially windy day the men made a fantastic sight as they went about their jobs with their heads bundled in scarves and wraps. They moved with their spades and wheelbarrows like so many myrmidons, shuttling from the trench to the dump where they dropped the tons of earth that had to be moved in order that the huge gash in the hill could be widened and deepened.

Thunderstorms often swept down without warning, to force an end to the work for the day and to wipe out a week's efforts by causing dangerous landslides. Heinrich had to invent safety devices and methods of shoring up the earthworks as they moved along. He was pioneering in the most ambitious campaign of excavation any one man had attempted. There was a single way to meet emergencies: by the trial-and-error method of the pioneer and the experimenter.

He grew short-tempered and desperately tired. There was illness among the workers. Next year he would need a doctor for them. Many of them were careless and a few dishonest. Suppose they were to find gold objects—he might never know if they sneaked off with them!

One week a gang dug into the breeding ground of thousands of poisonous snakes. Ten of the men threw dow their spades in horror and quit Hissarlik for good and all.

Dust, a merciless sun, myriads of stinging insects, and the whining, unrelenting wind . . . the summer was coming on too fast, the work proceeding at snail's pace. What Heinrich needed to find was unarguable proof that somewhere within this hillside lay the walls the Greeks had besieged for ten eventful years. Let him just touch these, and enclosed in them—nothing could persuade him otherwise—he would find treasure as well as the key to one of history's most fascinating puzzles.

He hired more laborers, and in May they began operations on a second large trench, this time on the south side. Each morning he arose confident that the day would bring the evidence he was hunting—a handful of bronze coins, or a fragment of armor. Each night he went to bed unrewarded but unshaken in his hope that tomorrow would finally be rewarding.

Worst of all were the echoes of unfriendly laughter that started to reach him from across the seas. European scholars who were hostile to the Hissarlik-Troy theory said that he was a lunatic, wasting time and money in an insane gamble. They were ready to discredit whatever he might find before he had found anything. They criticized his book, *Ithaca, the Peloponnesus, and Troy*. He himself admitted to Calvert that parts of it had been written in such a flush of excitement after his first survey of Hissarlik that he had made some rather extravagant statements. Later, he promised himself, he would retract a number of these claims and revise the entire book. Meanwhile his irritation mounted with every setback and delay on the site.

How easy it was, Heinrich often said to Sophie, to doubt instead of believe! How simple for those scholars, snug in their book-lined studies, to write disparagingly of his backbreaking labor on the hill. The only enterprise they showed was in digging up new arguments from old books to prove their stale theory that Troy was a myth. Well, let them go on theorizing! He was brown and wind-burned from the sun beating down on what no man could prove was *not* the soil of sacred Troy. He was somewhat discouraged, but his faith in the ultimate outcome was as stubborn as ever. It would take longer than he thought, that was all. Sophie often said, when he was moody, "Ah, Heinrich, how long has there been a Troy?"

"But you know as well as I! Better than two thousand years, my Sophie. Perhaps three."

"And how long have you worked and dreamed to come here?"

"Better than forty years, and you know it as well as I."

"Then we can afford," she would say softly, "to make haste slowly. Look how long it took my ancestors to storm the gates of Troy!"

And because by now the lines of strain and tension on his face had eased a little, she would reach for his copy of Homer and read, her voice and the musical words completing the spell her gentleness could work on him.

XV

"... and now the fire is heard more loudly through
the city, and the flames roll their flood of fire closer.
'Now come, dear father, climb on my back. I will
bear you on my shoulders and the weight will not be
too great a burden.'"

Aeneas, to his father. *Aeneid*, II, 705-709

In June they began in earnest to work Frank Calvert's
property on the steep northern slope. The digging had
barely started when their spades came upon the ruins of a
temple. Drums of Doric columns were uncovered after
their long burial. Then one gang discovered an ornamental
marble frieze on which Phoebus Apollo drove the four
horses of the Sun. To Heinrich it was evidence that he was
exploring the old Greek city of Novum Ilium, which had
been at its height long after Homer's Troy was over-
thrown.

The foundations of this temple could not be sharply de-
fined. A deep trench was sunk into the center of the
ruins, and to his amazement Heinrich began to discover a
veritable maze of ancient walls, one seemingly built on another, many leaning at wild angles, and each different in
age and style of masonry. The oldest wall rested on what
seemed to be virgin soil. He guessed that he must be touching the outer wall of the first city erected on Hissarlik.

Now stepping up the pace of the work, he brought in enormous windlasses and iron levers to loosen the hard debris of the lowest layer. He drove himself and his men tirelessly, and then he had to restrain his desire to push ahead so fast: a mass of hardened debris collapsed and buried two workmen alive. Fifty men clawed at the earth to save them. They were rescued, but it was a warning to proceed more slowly and to take wise precautions.

June was harvesting season for the local farmers. To keep his men on the job, Heinrich raised wages generously. More tools were needed; he invested in them and in horse carts. Disposing of the dirt removed from the trenches was increasingly difficult. As the size of the cuts increased, so did the dimensions of the dump and the length of the trips his men had to make with the barrowloads of dirt. The prevailing winds settled in the north, as they usually did after April. They blew skittishly over the dump area, picked up the powdery dust, and flung it back over the workmen. From sunrise to darkness the antlike columns of men filed back and forth, endlessly back and forth with their carts and barrows, crisscrossing the mound where several shafts and trenches were being worked simultaneously.

And then in the southern end of the largest trench Heinrich unearthed two distinct walls, each about fifteen feet broad, standing close together and grounded on what appeared to be solid bedrock. He called Calvert in for frequent conferences. As the flying picks and trundling barrows revealed the extent of these foundations, Heinrich would hardly leave the site long enough to eat.

"Now, Calvert," he said, "I wonder what my revered

colleagues will say! It looks to me like the foundation of a great tower."

"Then you believe you've reached Homeric Troy?"

"I am not prepared to say that—not yet. But I am prepared for laughter." His tone was ironic. "Of course it will be very *learned* laughter."

But Calvert had not seen him so optimistic for months. Without question this was the most formidable discovery so far, the base of a noble structure.

The Schliemanns had planned to winter in the stone hut, for it was much warmer and better built than the wooden house. The cold went to the very marrow of their bones; it was a rare day when "the blasts of Boreas" did not roar across Hissarlik. A few workmen stayed on throughout the winter months. Their clothing was so poor, however, and they suffered so keenly, that Heinrich and Sophie turned over to them their own stone house and moved back into the frame building, which was heated only by a fireplace.

Water left standing by the hearth in their room was always frozen by morning. But Heinrich would not leave. He counted the days to spring, using high wages, threats, cajolery, pleas, to keep his men on the job.

One midnight he was suddenly wakened, he did not know by what. There was a sullen red glare, and he smelled smoke. The wooden floor was ablaze. He roused Sophie with a cry, threw her coat about her, and pushed her outside. His shouting brought the foreman on the run. They tore up the floor with pickaxes and tamped earth on it. The planks had caught fire from sparks spat out of the grate. When it was over Heinrich was unnaturally silent. Only by the merest chance had he wakened soon enough.

With the coming of 1873 their second year's work was well under way. The second year! In moments of deliberate stock-taking, Heinrich had to confess that they still had found little but promising traces of the settlement he wanted to uncover. The great tower, yes; and fortification walls that seemed to circle a very early settlement; and countless thousands of pottery fragments, stone implements, and peculiar whorls made of glazed pottery, whose purpose he did not understand. But treasure? Warriors' helmets? Swords and gems? Golden cups?

His moods were protean. A fresh discovery made his hopes and spirits soar. Delays and frustrations exasperated him and he would lapse into gloomy silences. Once in a while he would come upon something that charmed him for the sudden glimpse it permitted into the shadowy past. Today, for instance, in one of the lower strata he had uncovered a few sun-dried bricks. One of them contained the crisp footprints of a dog, made while the clay was still moist, thousands of years ago. He called Sophie to come see it, and her quick delighted laughter made him smile for the first time in many days.

The expense of the project was staggering. Heinrich's most sympathetic friends wrote counseling him to stop now and be content with the fine Greek ruins he had brought up from the earth of Hissarlik. He brushed aside their advice. But he was concerned; a small fortune had gone into these trenches, and so far what had he to show for it? Nevertheless, a new trench was sunk in February, when a hundred and fifty-eight laborers were back on the site. His hope quickly skyrocketed, because he found well-hewn limestone walls and three inscriptions by which he could identify them as belonging to a temple of Athena. Again, this was a building of Hellenic origin, probably the most important sanctuary of all the temples of Novum Ilium.

When the Greeks took Troy at the climax of their long war, a black time followed. They put the torch to Priam's city and razed it to the ground. Heinrich never could forget this all the time that he worked in the complex of ruined houses and wrecked walls. He assured himself that when he touched the stratum of original Troy, there would be signs of fire, and by these signs he would know that the end of his search was nearing.

He was up one morning very early, walking among the temple ruins, mulling over a decision that he must make before his foreman arrived. Should he give orders to his men to stop where they were, and keep the ruins intact, or sacrifice them by ordering the workers to tunnel under and through them in the hope of finding more ancient remains?

This was the sort of choice he had to make day in and day out. Archeology was not an exact science. It would be several decades before field workers developed methods of measuring, photographing, and preserving materials so that such discoveries as Heinrich had to sacrifice could be preserved. In his eagerness to reach what he was avid to find he sometimes was destructive, though it did not seem so to him in his present frame of mind.

He saw his overseer and gave the order: *Dig deeper.* Only a few sections of the temple walls were left standing.

He believed himself fully justified in this decision when a house of nine rooms was found beneath the temple. Its size suggested that it had belonged to a powerful prince or chieftain. Near it were quantities of human bones and the skeletons of two warriors wearing fragments of bronze helmets. Their age? Their origin? He could not say. But finding the big house was a matter for quiet rejoicing. *Dig deeper*, he ordered, and the imperious tone of his voice rallied the men.

They discovered even more houses in the layer beneath. Each had been through fire, a frightful conflagration, apparently. At this depth almost everything showed signs of having been burned in a general disaster. Heinrich was outwardly calm, but Sophie knew his inner exultation. This appeared to be a whole city, *a city ravaged by fire*.

In March he began a large excavation close to their living quarters. At considerable depth were masses of partly vitrified bricks. Huge storage jars, taller than a man, still stood upright in their places. Everywhere were traces of ash. Droplets of glass told with what melting heat the fire had swept through this settlement. They discovered and cleared a steep, winding paved street. At its northern end was a double gateway, and embedded in the stone portals were huge copper bolts.

Calvert, their frequent and most welcome visitor, marveled at the size of the gate and its well-preserved bolts. Heinrich waited tensely for him to appraise this newest find. Hissarlik was deserted. It was evening, and for a long while there was a dramatic silence, except for the steady rhythm of Heinrich's walking stick tap-tap-tapping against his boot.

"I believe I can read your thoughts," Calvert said at last,

"because in the light of this we may have to discard the theory about the great tower."

"What do you think we have found?" asked Heinrich.

"The Scaean Gate, my friend. I believe that you have found the ruins of the Scaean Gate. The true great tower flanked this gate. Am I right? Is that your thought?"

"That is my thought. The other—I shall continue to call it the great tower. But this—yes, I am convinced that this is the Scaean Gate. Troy had many towers. But the position of this gateway agrees with Homer's description of the main one." In his eyes was the same look that had been in them that Christmas Day in Ankershagen long ago. He had thrown his last doubt and hesitation to the winds.

Calvert said in awe, "The Scaean Gate!" and into their minds moved a procession of the heroic figures who had passed through that famed gateway and into legend. This was the gate near which Hector bid farewell to his wife Andromache and removed his helmet when his baby son cried out, frightened by the sun dazzle on its bronze and the trembling of its bright horsehair plume. Aeneas had fled the burning city through this gate, carrying on his shoulders his old father while his small son trudged at his side.

"I think there will be less laughter now," Calvert said quietly, sharing his friend's tranquil mood.

"There may be laughter," Heinrich said. "I suppose there will always be laughter. But it will be hard to hear, behind these walls in windy Troy!"

XVI

"He carried with him much fine treasure from the spoils of Troy, while we, who have been on the same expedition, come home empty-handed."
His comrades, whispering about Odysseus.
Odyssey, X, 40-42

Heinrich ordered his gangs to stop clearing the flagstoned street when he saw that exposing more of it would demolish the walls of the chief's house. He had begun to talk about this structure as the "king's house," and finally, because he was so sure of having found the Scaean Gate nearby, it became "Priam's house" in his conversation.

Sophie had seldom seen him like this, almost boyishly confident, full of energy and gusto and drive. She observed that as his confidence deepened, he moved with greater deliberateness than before. This was because he was planning the formal announcement of his momentous findings. To an uninformed visitor on the site it might seem that the more than two years of work on Hissarlik had disclosed only a confused maze of ruins, many standing one atop the other in crazy disarray. But Heinrich and Sophie agreed with Frank Calvert that it was nearly time for a public announcement of their discovery of Troy.

Almost against his will Heinrich was being forced to use methods of greater precision in the work of excavating.

His first soaring enthusiasm was tempered; the amateur was being reshaped into a man of more patient techniques. It was not possible, he now knew, to study one stratum lying tidily above another and announce, "This one is Troy, and that one is Hellenic Ilium." Ancient peoples had not obliged him by building walls and houses in neat, logical sequence. He could not ticket and number them with the precision his orderly mind yearned for. Nature had contributed her own confusing touches to the mammoth puzzle. Earthquakes and landslides, centuries of eroding winds and rains, had left their marks. On this hilltop men had built their villages and towns, then rebuilt them haphazardly following devastating earthquake or fire. No single key would unlock the total mystery for him. In his diary Heinrich wrote down an account of each day's work, and on the site he began to preserve as much as possible of every ruin so that his statements about them could not be challenged. He was far more methodical than he had been at the outset.

All through March the evenings were noisy with the croaking of millions of frogs in the river marshes of the plain. Storks flapped overhead and built their nests on Troy. Screech owls made the night raucous; they liked the newly dug trenches for nesting places, and their eerie cries kept up until dawn.

In May Heinrich concentrated on the task of determining the exact limits of what he now called the Burnt City, the third one counting upward from the bedrock of Hissarlik. He believed that this was Troy of the *Iliad*. Everywhere in this layer were signs of fire. He sank twenty shafts in strategic places, and because he found nothing but sherds of Hellenic pottery, he was satisfied that the walls of Homeric Troy did not extend beyond the original plateau of Hissarlik, while the later city of New Troy had sprawled out beyond it. The hilltop itself, he was sure, had served in later years as an acropolis.

He felt himself to be very close to answering the questions disputed by scholars for generations. He hastened the tempo of the digging everywhere, especially on the north and the south. Meanwhile, the picture of how human life had been lived here became in some respects more clear and, in other respects, more confused. He could make out the remains of five different prehistoric settlements on the hill. Their inhabitants had not often troubled to remove the debris of old buildings when they constructed new ones. No wonder it was such a baffling problem! Or they had dumped their rubbish over one side of the plateau, thus changing its size and shape from the original contours. But the more he made visible, the more certain Heinrich was that the Burnt City, third from the bottom, was Homer's Troy.

The yield of all the different shafts and trenches was unrewarding for the next several weeks, and from his point of view, not especially interesting. Sophie was called to Athens by the death of her father. Heinrich missed her. Without her cheering companionship he gave way to depression. As matters stood, he had poured a small fortune into these operations, and it would be quite possible to see most of his money go. He had driven himself unstintingly; he felt physically exhausted.

He searched his heart. Had he not done archeology a tremendous service, he wondered. What he had found was not treasure, except in the sense that its continuing study would enrich man's knowledge of the past. But all his life he had dreamed of making a spectacular discovery. Without some last sensational finding to crown the years of labor he would never feel entirely recompensed. Troy had been a princely capital. Why had he failed to turn up princely jewels or golden coins? It must be, he decided with resignation, that the treasure houses had been plundered and their hoards stolen in ancient days. He would have to console himself with having proved that Troy did exist because he had uncovered its burned ruins. With these conclusions reluctantly reached, Heinrich made up his mind to suspend operations in June. Mycenae might be more fruitful of actual gold or treasure to show a skeptical world. It was a painful decision to make.

When she returned early in June, Sophie expressed no regret over his decision. Life on Troy was anything but comfortable, although she never complained. She began packing their valises.

For the next several days the workers' spades uncovered more and more Hellenic and pre-Hellenic ruins. A new and previously undetected circuit wall was found. Heinrich studied this with the closest attention. One hot morning he was supervising a gang of men digging just to the northwest of the great gate and near "Priam's house" when he saw the spade of a workman touch the lip of an oddly shaped copper container. Within it something glittered in the morning sun. His throat suddenly tightened; the copper lay beneath a layer of burned material, and even his quick eye had nearly missed seeing it.

"Sophie!" he called, his voice tense. She was instantly at

his side. "Tell the men it is time for *paidos*." This was the Turkish word for a rest period.

"But Heinrich," she said, "they've hardly begun to work!"

She had never heard him speak so sharply. "Tell them I had forgotten that today is my birthday," he commanded. "Tell them anything! They are to have the whole day off at full wages. Quickly! Dismiss them. The foreman, too. See that every man leaves the hill."

"Yes, Heinrich. At once."

Her face showed astonishment, but she acted rapidly. When she had made sure that the last man was gone, she returned to find Heinrich hacking away at something wedged beneath the stones of a massive wall. At every stroke the boulders threatened to topple and cave in on him, but he was oblivious of danger. She knelt beside him without a word, and her strong fingers went to work too. Piece by piece Heinrich and Sophie began to lift out objects of many sizes and shapes. All were packed tightly together in a rectangular mass. Once they must have been buried in a wooden chest, but the wood had long since been eaten away by the forces of decay. Only something that looked like a copper key remained of it. Heinrich pried it out. "Look!" he exclaimed, and held it up for her to see, his face working with emotion, and then he went back to his digging with a knife and with his hands until his fingertips cracked and bled. They lost track of time.

When they reached the end of the hoard, they had dug out thousands upon thousands of objects. Most were made of gold. Sophie put them in her shawl and made many trips with them to the frame house. When Heinrich was satisfied that nothing more remained, they stood with their arms about each other in the hut, marveling at the beauty of the beads, the hairpins, the necklaces and diadems, and the goblets and cups of ancient electrum and silver. A shimmer of light playing over the golden trinkets made them seem as shining and unstained as though the Trojan smith had finished polishing them yesterday.

Heinrich and Sophie clung to each other and laughed, and then they wept. His fingers trembled when he selected a gold headdress of exquisite workmanship and placed it on her brow.

"You shall wear a queen's jewels," he told her. "The golden ornaments of Helen of Troy!"

His triumph was hers. "You have found the treasure of Priam, Heinrich. The world has much to marvel over, thanks to you!"

XVII

"Neither glory nor honor spring from those **who** run away."
> Ajax, encouraging the Greeks to battle.
> *Iliad*, XV, 564

So the dream was realized. He could walk Troy's streets and gaze down on the plain of the River Scamander, fair now with its fields of red and yellow summer flowers. He could hold reverently in his own hands the golden treasure of King Priam. What more could life promise? A man of smaller faith might have said, "Nothing." But Heinrich had fresh campaigns to plan. That other treasures were still imprisoned in hidden tombs and were awaiting his discovery he did not doubt.

Meanwhile, with his passion to weave together all details and make them dovetail exactly with Homer's stories, he worked out a theory to explain the miracle of the treasure-trove: Troy had been under fatal attack. Someone, acting in frantic haste, packed the hoard into a wooden chest and carried it from the king's house but neglected to remove the key. He had managed to reach the city wall. Then something halted him—a flung javelin, an arrow, or perhaps the fire. He dropped the chest by the wall and there it lay unseen, to be covered by ash and stone when the nearby house tumbled to destruction.

Small wonder that for Sophie and Heinrich the words of Homer sang with new meanings. One of the silver vases of their collection contained nearly 8,700 objects, mostly beads of purest gold. Heinrich blessed the presence of mind of that unknown fugitive who had set the vase upright in the chest. That was why nothing had spilled out. Two silver dishes had been broken, but a third was undamaged. The large copper vessel, which had been the first thing to catch his eye, had projected outward in such a way that it protected the bulk of the treasure.

Sophie and Heinrich worked together to classify and count their hoard. Besides the small golden objects such as the earrings, buttons, goblets, bracelets and armlets, chains and ornaments, there were silver talents and curiously shaped plates. There were copper and bronze battle-axes, daggers and helmet crests, and a whole shield made of copper. The most wonderful of the headdresses, the one he loved to place on Sophie, contained a total of 16,353 chains, rings, and delicate leaves of gold, suspended by fine gold wires.

Heinrich was content to stop further excavation on the seventeenth of June. What he liked to call "the criticism of his pickaxe and spade" had armed him to answer the doubters. So Troy was myth, was it? He would display its jewels to his critics. He would invite them to study the shield with a boss very like those described in the *Iliad*, and fragments of cunningly made helmets. He personally would escort them through the flagstoned, windswept streets.

Always he had believed in the exactness of Homer's words, and the world would now hear how faith was justified. He was so confident of fortune's smiling face that he began to plan the expedition in Mycenae to hunt for the tombs of Agamemnon and the warrior chiefs.

Before this journey, however, Heinrich published the first account of his Trojan discoveries. The book was brought out in English, French, and German editions. Furious attacks from European scholars greeted its publication. He had known it would be attacked, but he was wholly unprepared for the pettiness of some of the faultfinding. In all charity he had to blame some of the tirades on jealousy.

One day Frank Calvert found him stamping about on the hill, leafing through an article in a magazine that had just reached him.

"Read this!" he ordered, livid with anger. "It's past belief! How could anyone stoop to such slander?"

Calvert skimmed it quickly, then said with distaste, "I agree, this is unpardonable."

The author of the article hinted with heavy sarcasm that everything Heinrich claimed to have found on Hissarlik had been put there deliberately, presumably by Heinrich, to create sensational publicity for himself.

What most galled the conventional scholars was that Heinrich was an amateur and that he presumed to speak as an authority.

All right! He had a temper, too! He was capable of answering with as much heat as his critics gave off, and he was a match for them in a dozen languages.

Despite the criticism, some of which was vicious and some merely silly, people throughout the civilized world read his reports avidly and were stirred. His book with its two hundred pictures created a sensation. Any man or woman who had read Homer or heard of the *Iliad*, everyone who had learned the old legends about Troy, was captured by the romance of the Schliemann expedition and its findings. His book was most seriously studied in England and America. The German scholars who read *Troy and Its Remains* were bound to the tradition that only a trained student had the right to be authoritative, and they gave him a bad time. At least, no one who heard of the Trojan adventure was indifferent or neutral. People everywhere were curious about Heinrich and his theories, his plans, his methods, his life and thoughts. Lay people if not scholars waited hopefully for him to conquer new worlds of the ancient past. The grocer's apprentice was internationally famous. And fame made him all the more stubborn and aggressive in his replies to the charge that he had made unprovable claims.

The time was to come when he would have to revise many of his theories, but now Heinrich rode the crest of the wave. He was to go back to Hissarlik with a small army of trained scientists to check and recheck his claims and coldly question his own hasty conclusions. He would have architects and draftsmen, photographers, engineers, and a host of technicians to take the place of his inspired hunches and poetic insights. But that lay in the future. He had done the bold path-breaking job of the pioneer, and his success made him deeply angry with his detractors.

The wintry month of February, 1874, saw him bring workmen to the rocky acropolis of Mycenae, thought to be the most ancient city of Greece, for the first campaign on that site. Thirty-four vertical trial shafts were sent down before the work had to be halted because of difficulties with the Greek government. Restrictions were clamped on Heinrich as to the number of men he might employ and where he could dig. Officials insisted that there had to be government overseers on the site at all times.

His quarrel with the Greek authorities grew out of their ruling that any treasure he found must automatically become government property. Heinrich felt that because it was his money and his time and labor being expended, he should be allowed to keep whatever his spades uncovered for the duration of his lifetime. This was the first of many tussles he was to have with officials both here and in the Troad. A strict watch had been put over his activities ever since he had impulsively spirited away the great treasure from Troy. Beyond question this had been a willful act, the act of a man who disliked and mistrusted authority and its arbitrary decisions. He reasoned, rightly or wrongly, that what he had found belonged to him to do with as he wished; he planned eventually to donate all his trophies to a museum of his choice. But the Turkish government was outraged, and the Greek government intended not to be placed in a similar position.

Finally Heinrich got his grant of permission to work the area of the acropolis. Other searchers still occasionally explored the ground outside the acropolis, but he was of the opinion that they could dig forever and find nothing. He was guiding himself by the old geographer Pausanias, who, about 170 A.D., had written:

The Argives (or northern Greeks) pulled down Mycenae because of envy. For while the Argives were inactive in the face of the Persian expedition, the Mycenaeans sent eighty men to Thermopylae who shared the glory of the Lacedaemonians. This desire for fame brought destruction to the Mycenaeans by irritating the Argives. Still left of the city, however, are parts of the wall, including the gate on which lions stand guard. These beasts are said to be the work of the Cyclopes, the same people who constructed the wall at Tiryns for Proteus. In the remains of Mycenae is a fountain called Persea; also there are the underground buildings in which the treasure of Atreus and his children was stored. A tomb of Atreus is there, as well as the graves of those who came home with Agamemnon from Troy, who were murdered by Aegisthus after he had given them a banquet. The tomb of Cassandra is argued about by the Lacedaemonians who live around Amyclae. Different is the tomb of Agamemnon, the one of Eurymedon, his charioteer, and still another shared by Teledamus and Pelops—for they say Cassandra bore these twin sons, and while they were babies Aegisthus killed them with their parents—and the tomb of Electra, whom Orestes gave in marriage to Pylades. Hellanicus notes that the children Medon and Strophius were born of Electra to Pylades. Clytemnestra and Aegisthus were buried a little beyond the wall, for they were thought unworthy of a place within its enclosure where lay Agamemnon and those who were murdered with him.

Pausanias, *Description of Greece*,
"Corinth," II, xvi, 5-7

Who was he, Heinrich often thought, to turn his back on Pausanias as other excavators had done? They were misinterpreting the passage, he was sure; by "the wall,"

Heinrich was positive that Pausanias referred to the inner wall of the acropolis, while other archeologists thought he meant the circuit wall of the city. Thus they had concluded that Pausanias located the five tombs in the lower city and the tombs of Clytemnestra and Aegisthus outside it. Heinrich was convinced that they were utterly mistaken.

His literal interpretation of passages in Homer had led him to phenomenal success at Troy—while scholars made fun of him. Now he would follow his enlightened hunch about the words of Pausanias. Down went the shafts inside the old acropolis, which stood to the southwest of the Lion Gate.

Delay followed delay. He was annoyed by further legal proceedings which halted his work until April of 1876. Not until then could he resume operations at Mycenae. And he was ordered to pay the Turkish government an indemnity of £400 and turn back half his Trojan treasure.

Heinrich now indulged in one of the grand gestures he dearly loved: he sent not £400, but £2,000 to the Turkish Minister of Public Instruction, asking that it be used for the benefit of the Imperial Museum. He also filed an application for permission to dig again at Troy in the near future.

The shafts at Mycenae went deeper and a full-scale campaign was at last under way. Heinrich was probing the ruins of the city to which Agamemnon, king of men, leader of all the Argive chiefs, returned after the sacking and burning of Troy. Here he was slain by his wife Clytemnestra, who never had ceased to grieve because he had sacrificed their daughter Iphigenia to make the gods grant a favoring wind and speed the Greek fleet on its way to Troy. Her lover Aegisthus helped with the murder. Here, fresh from their Trojan victory, Agamemnon and his followers died after a gaudy banquet. Tradition said they had been laid in their graves amid pomp and splendor and with golden treasure around them.

Within the enclosure of the old acropolis Heinrich believed that he would find the tombs that had been undiscovered for centuries.

"Dig deeper!" he ordered his men. "We need more shafts. Another trench! Dig deeper! We waste time!" Sophie recognized that tone of voice. Heinrich would let nothing hinder him now.

XVIII

"O resourceful and bold Odysseus, what greater
work than this can you plan in your heart?"
Achilles to Odysseus in Hades.
Odyssey, XI, 473-474

"You are to form three work parties," Heinrich told his
foremen. "One will dig here, near the Lion Gate, and clear
the passageway into what used to be the acropolis. The
second is to work about forty feet from here." He pointed
to a stake in the ground. "A trench will go there. Every
potsherd and any object, no matter how small, is to be reported at once. The third gang will excavate the south
side of the treasury near the Lion Gate." The men working
in the vicinity of the gateway, he knew, would have the
hardest going. When the city was stormed ages ago, its
defenders hurled boulders from the walls upon the attack-
ing forces below, and those rocks still choked the passageway.

He turned back to Sophie while the work gangs went
about their tasks. "So, we have begun." She had been resting in the shade, but arose now to take charge of the diggers working near the treasury, which was her own special assignment. Mycenae to her seemed as arid as the hill
of Hissarlik had once appeared. It was pasture land pierced
with cliffs and steep slopes. The old town had been a mecca

for famous travelers from time out of mind. Pausanias was a late-comer when he reported what he had seen here. Even to him the city wall must have been a quaint ruin.

From its very start the digging showed rich promise. Beneath the comparatively recent Hellenic city they found thousands of fragments of archaic vases, ornamented in a profusion of colors. Terra-cotta idols cropped up, and playful little animal figures. Many of the strange terra-cotta whorls found at Troy were turning up here too. Heinrich guessed that the small ones were once strung together as necklaces, because many of them were perforated. The larger could have served as weights to hold a spindle steady in spinning. At the north end of one trench he brought to light a water conduit that showed its builders to have been highly proficient engineers.

From the same trench came a tombstone, and then a second, sculptured with bas-reliefs of charioteers in hunting scenes. The chariots were very like the type Homer describes. Heinrich fairly purred with pleasure. Such finds as these were enormously gratifying.

Each day's work brought him assurance that they were on the right track. In another trench they excavated a wall of upright stone slabs. They were working *inside* the circuit wall of the city. Near the upright stones were masses of pottery fragments and idols of the goddess Hera, very ancient objects indeed. Two more gravestones were found. Every discovery quickened Heinrich's expectations. The presence of tombs this close to the Lion Gate was significant: he could recall no historic example of an acropolis serving as a burial place, with the exception of the building of the Caryatids in the Acropolis at Athens, for the acropolis of any city was its elevated fortress zone. What most satisfied him and sped him on was the discovery of this inner wall. This must be the one to which Pausanias referred; it must circle the ancient acropolis, and somewhere in this sacred area must be the tombs of people important enough for the honor of burial in consecrated ground.

One morning a foreman brought him a square, heavy object of deep red color. "This has just been found, sir. It seems undamaged."

Heinrich turned it over in his hands. "Good!" he said, rubbing its surface with his thumb. He looked highly pleased. "Excellent!"

The foreman hesitated. "What do you make of it, Mr. Schliemann? It doesn't appear of much value."

Heinrich said, "No. Intrinsically it has slight value. This is red granite. It is a die, used by a goldsmith or silversmith."

Not gold, but the hint that they might be close to it: a mold with impressions for casting earrings. Where they found the tools of workers in precious metal they should be able to find examples of their handcraft, too.

Every night Heinrich pondered the words of Pausanias. When that writer visited Mycenae, the tombstones of the heroes' graves were already lost under layers of soil at least eight feet in depth. Four centuries before the date of Pausanias's trip, the city had been a shambles.

Soon after finding the mold, they turned up a gold-plated button. Heinrich fingered it thoughtfully, his eyes aglow. Then came a sizable cache of bronze: five knives, two lances, and double-edged hatchets . . . ever richer and finer, now, the objects they unearthed. Onyx and agate gems with intaglios of animals, and of unsurpassed crafts-manship, drifted to the surface.

Together with Sophie he superintended the work from dawn until the light failed. It was Hissarlik all over again. The sun was scorching and the dust a torture to their weary eyes. But they were happy and hopeful, for as Heinrich recorded in his notes, "Nothing more interesting can be imagined than the excavation of a prehistoric city of immortal glory, where nearly every object, even to the fragments of pottery, reveals a new page of history."

The weather was good: hot, but clear. Sophie was in full charge of the men at work on the beehive-shaped building which they thought to be a treasury. Later they decided it was a tomb, and eventually it came to be called the tomb of Clytemnestra. Sophie had thirty laborers and two horse carts under her personal direction. The job was heavy and went slowly because of the stones that had fallen from the building's vault.

Heinrich was everywhere at once, bubbling with energy and hard put to it to conceal his mounting excitement. One trench and a shaft were particularly fertile. Experience had taught him to control his bursts of enthusiasm, but of course he had to dash from one end of the acropolis to the other a hundred times a day to see how the work was progressing everywhere.

The threshold of the Lion Gate was finally cleared. He and Sophie saw that its base of immense slabs was scored so that beasts of burden passing through it would have firm footing. In the beehive tomb Sophie discovered traces of beautifully ornamented friezes. In the acropolis they had dug to prehistoric debris in which they picked out knives of opal and arrows of obsidian. Inside the ruins of an early house were many precious ornaments. One was a ring cut out of white onyx, with delicate intaglio representations of animals.

"How lovely!" Sophie, who had just finished cleaning it, slipped it on her finger admiringly. "It is very old, Heinrich."

"Of much greater age than anything we have found, Sophie."

"It makes one see that Homer was not necessarily exaggerating," she mused, "in his description of the shield of Achilles!"

But by far the most promising of these sites was the area where the sculptured tombstones rested. Here Heinrich came upon black ashes one day. He lifted out a bone button covered with gold, and an ivory imitation of a ram's horn. Many other objects bore the hooked cross, or swastika, that so often occurred on the pottery and gold pieces he had found at Troy.

The heavy rains of December stopped their work and transformed the trenches into rivers of mud. They were working eleven feet down. It was frustrating to be kept indoors and have to watch the rain beat on such productive ground.

Then came better weather. At twenty-five feet below the surface Heinrich reached a stone-walled tomb. Spaced only three feet from each other, and beneath a layer of pebbles, were the remains of three human bodies. They had been burned where they lay, on funeral pyres, it seemed. Distinct marks of fire and smoke had stained the stone walls of their tomb. Heinrich reminded Sophie of certain ancient ceremonial rites: small pebbles were often strewn about the corpses in order to ventilate cremation fires.

Each body was crowned with a diadem of thin gold plate executed by a master artisan. And all were surrounded by treasure. As Heinrich reached out eager hands to lift several of the objects, a couple of them fell apart and their powder blew away in his fingers. He thought them to be cylinders of Egyptian glass, so old that they vanished at the breath of air.

Due south of these graves workmen were finding some more large steles, or tombstones. Beneath them were horizontal stone slabs. Pottery and many small obsidian knives indicated that the graves were prehistoric. Here, as in the first grave, were three bodies laden with gold plate. Heinrich silently and with wonder lifted disc after disc of pure gold from its hiding place. He supposed that these were miniature replicas of shields, designed to ornament clothing. Some were circular; others were incised in the form of leaves.

This was a story of triumph, as it had been at Hissarlik, but with a difference: here at Mycenae there were bodies, and it was possible to observe how the ceremonial burial rites had been performed. One almost felt himself present at a hero's funeral. The tombs contained many jewels engraved with pictures that captured thrilling moments in the hunt and in games and battles. The work of unknown artisans came out of the earth to speak of the skill of men who thousands of years ago were moved by beauty and put their impressions of it on imperishable metals and gems. Which was more wonderful—the twenty-five-inch crown of pure gold, or the onyx finger-ring bearing the figure of a graceful leaping deer? Which better befitted royalty: the silver scepters or the bits of sparkling rock crystal that once had been a noble basin?

And yet it was only the beginning of the overwhelming discoveries. A primitive funeral altar showed Heinrich that on a spot undisturbed since the burials took place he had come upon a truly majestic tomb. Five huddled bodies were found, three lying with their heads to the east and two with their heads to the north.

They were heavily laden with jewelry and gold ornament. Tripods, of the sort that were prizes in the Olympic games . . . golden buttons in vast numbers . . . a bull's head of silver with two long golden horns . . . lances whose wooden shafts crumbled away when air touched them . . . masks of gold plate on the withered faces of the ancient dead. One had a youth's features, with a long Grecian nose and small expressive mouth. Another mask portrayed an older man with deep eyes and broad forehead. So pure was the gold, and so soft, that pieces ripped off and Heinrich was afraid even to handle them. Golden goblets and massive cups came out of the depths. On them, dramatic hunting scenes showed young men chasing lions. She-goats nursed their wobbly-legged kids in pictures cut into precious stones no larger than Sophie's fingernail.

Heinrich found and excavated, in all, five tombs at Mycenae. They lay in a great circle inside the walls of the old acropolis. Sometime later a sixth was found, although he stopped with the finding of the fifth tomb because Pausanias had said there were only five. All together sixteen or seventeen bodies were discovered; their condition made it hard to be positive about the number. Several were of high-born women and possibly children, wrapped in sheets of gold.

Heinrich's journal could hardly keep pace with the finds.

"I further found ten gold plates," he wrote one night. "I also collected not less than fifty-three golden cuttlefish . . . copper vessels . . . fillets of silver . . . forty-six bronze knives . . . traces of well-woven linen . . . amber beads and gold ribbons . . . grave ornaments . . ."

Each tomb was a storehouse of jewels and weapons and valuable metal objects.

Throughout the winter nights of 1877 watch fires burned on the acropolis of Mycenae. Not since the Argives had captured it—about 468 B.C.—had soldiers stood guard here. Now they were stationed near the circle graves to prevent illegal digging or thefts under cover of darkness.

The fifth tomb contained but one body. Heinrich made strenuous efforts to preserve its fragile skull, which was crowned with a golden headdress and on which was a gold mask. He asked—with a new touch of humility that rather surprised his friends—for advice about preserving the shrunken and mummified bodies. No one could say. He hired an artist to make an oil painting of the last-found body because he knew, sadly, that it would be dust in a few days' time, and he was willing to experiment to the extent of letting a druggist from Argos pour over it a mixture of alcohol and gum sandarac, to harden it and perhaps ensure its preservation.

The acropolis of Mycenae was by this time a center of world attention. Curiosity seekers streamed in and peasants left their homes to gape at the stir and bustle as if a fair had set up its tents. Renowned scholars visited the site. One day Heinrich and Sophie were hosts to the Emperor of Brazil. Daily they greeted university students and professors whose neat theories were being turned topsy-turvy by Heinrich's Mycenaean discoveries. He was asked to lecture in England and France and to write for newspapers and popular magazines. It was beyond all imagining. First Troy, and now Mycenae.

In the telegrams announcing the Mycenean graves, he said, "I have discovered the tombs which tradition designates as those of Agamemnon, Cassandra, Eurymedon, and their companions." He did not say, "*I have found the actual tombs*," although what he said was quite different from what he believed. But he had been accused of letting theory get in the way of fact. He would give critics no new ground for attack.

Consequently the sternest of them were not quite so quick to dispute him. Agamemnon and his warriors might well have been buried with such barbaric splendor. These graves had been found where Pausanias said they were. When Heinrich spoke of the tombs of Agamemnon and Clytemnestra there was less scoffing, because the gold masks and armor of the Age of Heroes were dazzling evidence of a find of historic magnitude.

Sophie brought to an end the prodigious task of clearing most of the beehive tomb. As at Troy, she never once had asked special consideration or taken longer rest periods than the men. Of such an achievement any man could be proud, but she took small credit. Every time Heinrich called her she would instantly respond, wherever she was. Her full tiered skirt was usually grimy with dust. She would pull her tight-fitting little hat, bedraggled and dusty now though it came originally from Paris, more closely upon her head and hurry off to him, her velvet-edged jacket fluttering about her as she ran.

Sophie Schliemann modestly effaced herself. Heinrich wrote always of "my" work and "my" discoveries. Sophie did not write. She had babies. She cooked. She dug. She read Greek to him. She listened. She was at his shoulder whenever he needed her. Just as on the hill of Hissarlik, the last and most delicate digging by small knife and sensitive fingertips was done by her while she knelt in the dust and ash of the Shaft Graves.

But her softer light was not wholly eclipsed by his central sun. It burned steadily and gave out its radiance. The quarrels of scholars were of no moment to her, but the joy in her husband's face when he touched the warriors' masks meant far more to Sophie than the writing that would go on about them endlessly.

XIX

"Olympian Zeus himself brings happiness to all sorts of men as he so wills. To you he has given this trial, and you must therefore endure it."
Nausicaä to Odysseus. *Odyssey*, VI, 188-190

The son born to them in 1876 was given the name Agamemnon. Before the Christian rites of baptism in an Athens church, Heinrich gently held a copy of Homer against the head of his baby son and read aloud a hundred lines of the *Iliad*.

The preparation of a book about his discoveries at Mycenae had absorbed most of Heinrich's time for the past year, and he was kept busy also with the correspondence resulting from his other books. But he was becoming restless in Athens; desk work was never as satisfying as excavation. He wanted to return to Asia Minor. Operations should be reopened at Troy to answer many questions, some of them urgent. Charges had been made that he was unscientific in his methods and inaccurate in his conclusions about Hissarlik. Heinrich wanted fresh evidence to confirm his published statements about Troy, but he would have to wait until September of 1878 for official permission from the Turkish government before he could resume the work.

Meanwhile he acted on the plan he had made eight years

ago, before his spades had explored Troy, by journeying to Ithaca to excavate in this third region of myth and history. He made soundings in the valley of Polis, where tradition said that the ancient capital of Ithaca had stood, but he found nothing of a date earlier than the fifth century, B.C.

The fantastic luck that walked so often at his side seemed wayward this time. He tramped across various sites, hunting the ruins of old towns, but there were no epic-making discoveries and no thunderbolts of publicity to hurl from Ithaca. For the first time Heinrich used the word "failure" to describe a campaign. It came hard.

On the rocky summit where the "castle of Odysseus" stood he traced out some very old walls of cyclopean masonry. Here too he uncovered the chambers of a mansion, or of six or seven separate residences; he could not be sure just what he had found, and he was not hasty about deciding. A note of caution and deliberateness could be detected in all his statements. This mansion better suited his ideal of a Homeric palace than his so-called "king's house" at Troy. More carefully than ever before he preserved masses of pottery fragments for study so they might be compared with similar types found at Mycenae and Troy.

Until recent years archeologists had given only slight attention to potsherds. But two years before at Mycenae, Heinrich had decided that pottery could furnish revealing clues to the age of the places where it was found. He had fired off several angry telegrams to high officials, begging them to compel the Greek government's representative to stop pitching ceramic fragments over the cliffs along with other dump material. He called the man's action "vandal-ism," for he himself was now convinced, as he said, that pottery was "a cornucopia of archeological wisdom." His own work had demonstrated its value.

Any location with a place name that harked back to Homer always attracted him. He went to explore a small cave known as "the grotto of the nymphs" near the port in Ithaca where Odysseus landed and where with the help of flashing-eyed Athena he hid his wealth. Heinrich dug and searched and dug some more, but found no treasure. At length he gave it up and concentrated on plans for a fourth year's work at Troy.

This time they were to launch another full-scale cam-paign. In addition to the technicians in the group, ten armed police officers constantly stood guard against ban-dits and to protect Heinrich against thieving workmen. There had been a sorry experience in 1873 when two na-tives made off with several gold objects, melted them down, and thus destroyed irreplaceable treasure.

The principal excavation was on the site of the large building northwest of the "Scaean Gate," the one Hein-rich always preferred to call Priam's palace. In late Octo-ber three small hoards of treasure were brought up, and a large one of gold jewelry. Work had to stop with the heavy rains in November and it could not start again until the following March.

More conscientiously than before, and because of So-phie's concern, Heinrich was trying to take care of his health. Every morning he rose before dawn to ride his saddle horse to the Hellespont for a swim in its chill wa-ters. He was sure that the early morning bath and exercise accounted for his vigorous good health. But he was no longer a young man, and he humored Sophie by working less strenuously.

During the fifth year at Hissarlik two distinguished scientists joined his party. Prof. Rudolf Virchow of Berlin was a man of varied talents: an eminent physiologist, anthropologist, and research worker. The other newcomer was M. Émile Burnouf, who was Honorary Director of the French School of Archeology at Athens. Virchow studied the vegetation and the geology of the Plain of Troy. He was equally interested in the human and animal remains found within the settlements on Hissarlik. Also, being a doctor of medicine, he was able to treat illnesses among the staff and workmen. Burnouf was both an engineer and a draftsman. His maps and sketches were prepared with professional accuracy.

And during this campaign all measurements and surveys, as well as the disposal of debris, were expertly supervised. Heinrich smarted under the accusation that in bygone years he had been careless and destructive.

More streets were cleared. Foundation stones of other old houses were laid bare. Obviously, there were many dramatic discoveries still to be made. Heinrich branched out from Hissarlik to start operations on two large and four small tumuli, or burial mounds, located nearby on the Troad. In Virchow's company he walked about the plain exploring mounds and fragmentary ruins to which tradition gave imposing and romantic names. Together the two men climbed Mount Ida, although Heinrich was still feeling shaky because of a fall from his horse a short while earlier. They investigated all the places that held hints of ancient human living. Virchow measured and surveyed, and if Burnouf accompanied them, he sketched and painted.

Both these men made contributions to *Ilios*, the new book Heinrich was writing. It was published late in 1880. In it Virchow defended Heinrich against the worst charge his critics made—that he was destructive. About the early work on Hissarlik, Virchow wrote:

> "If you could see what mounds of earth (in the full sense of the word) had to be dug away and removed, in order to have a view of the lower layers, you would indeed scarcely believe that a single man in the course of a few years could have accomplished so great an undertaking. On this occasion I would stand up for Schliemann against a reproach which, although plausible in itself, falls to the ground on closer consideration —the reproach that he has not excavated from the surface, layer by layer, so as to obtain a complete plan for each sucessive period."

By the end of that year Hissarlik resembled a fortress. The once barren plateau was now, when one viewed it from the plain, like a citadel whose walls could be seen clearly even from a distance. To a visitor standing on the hill itself, the walls and foundations of the Burnt City appeared to lie at the bottom of a deep inverted funnel.

Virchow did not call the third settlement the Homeric city. He thought it *possible* the charred ruins might be this. And Heinrich was no longer insistent that they had to be sacred Ilios. He was restrained in his writings, even if in his heart he would not yet permit the flicker of a doubt.

When that year's campaign drew to a close, he did not know that it was to be his next to final one on the site. The fine work of his staff had impressed him. None of them was given to making snap judgments. They were trained men, scientists who used the word *possibly* more often than the word *certainly*. He was learning from them as well as from bitter personal experience. Their systematic methods replaced the amateurish approach to excavation which had served him in the first lonely and groping years.

The publication of his book *Ilios* poked up a proverbial hornets' nest. Burnouf's drawings showed that the buildings of the third city, counting upward from bedrock, were very simple structures, not at all as sumptuous as one might expect the mansions of nobility to be. Why, they were little better than rude huts, said the critics. How could anyone assert that this was mighty Troy? When Homer sang of the city, he described it as great and elegant. This man Schliemann, said several haughty European scholars, was laughable; he dug up a few miserable houses and some narrow streets and claimed preposterous things about them.

The worst of it was that Heinrich himself was beginning to feel doubtful. He had an explanation, but one that really did not satisfy him at all. "We must stop thinking of Troy," he would say over and over again, "as we do of a modern city." Of course its dimensions were small, and so were its houses; that was what the settlements of early man were like. But he was more and more a prey to secret gnawing doubts, which nibbled away at his confidence like little field mice in a granary.

Dr. Wilhelm Dörpfeld, an architect turned archeologist, joined the staff in 1881. After long, objective study of the ruins, he too began to dispute Heinrich's belief that the Burnt City was Homeric Troy. He was persuasive. And their most recent digging shook Heinrich's theory that the great tower was what he had thought, or that the "Scaean Gate" was anything more than the entrance to an ancient city fortress through which people had come and gone perhaps hundreds of years before Homer was born.

Yes, the new excavations were undermining Heinrich's theory about the Burnt City. Now his gangs were finding walls that belonged to buildings of massive dimensions; one was a dwelling place that was undeniably a palace. This resembled the lavish castle in Ithaca, which had measured up better than anything in the third city to Heinrich's idea of a nobleman's home.

All of this was naturally upsetting and troubling, but to make matters worse, the work slowed to an absolute standstill in March of 1882. Heinrich again was at loggerheads with the Turkish government, which kept a representative on the site at all times to superintend operations and to make sure that the country's interests were protected.

This man took an unreasonable attitude about phases of the work which he did not fully understand. When he saw Dr. Dörpfeld moving around with his surveying instruments, he informed the military governor of the Dardenelles that this party of industrious Germans seemed engaged in highly suspicious activities. Perhaps they were mapping plans of a nearby Turkish fortress. He volunteered his opinion that they were using the excavations at Hissarlik as a pretext for spying. Dörpfeld was commanded to stop using his surveying instruments. In a boiling fury Heinrich sent protests to the governor, but the representative stayed. This man assumed an even more pompous air once his hand was officially strengthened. "Just how, please, am I to tell the difference between Dr. Dörpfeld taking notes on fortifications and Dr. Dörpfeld making a survey?" he demanded. While the staff tried to carry out their daily assignments, the wrangle grew hotter. "Dr. Dörpfeld must therefore discontinue taking notes or doing any writing whatsoever. My government stands behind my decision."

Heinrich shot off volleys of indignant letters and complaints, but the government man was conscientious, no matter how ill-informed he might be about archeological techniques. "If Dr. Dörpfeld will not co-operate," he said blandly, "it will be my unpleasant duty to arrest Dr. Dörpfeld and ship him to Constantinople in chains. Dr. Dörpfeld would not enjoy the trip."

Finally Heinrich appealed to the German Embassy, explaining that the fortress on which they were suspected of spying was five miles away and that they wanted nothing except new plans of ancient Troy. He implored protection from such idiots, such *Dummköpfe!*

They were deadlocked for five months. In August Heinrich took the issue directly to Chancellor Bismarck. He was, he said, humiliated, insulted, slandered, persecuted. . . . After this, wheels began to turn. German diplomacy smoothed the way, and Dr. Dörpfeld was finally permitted to trundle his surveying equipment where he wished and to make notes as he needed. He finished drawing his plans in November. Eight whole months had been lost!

In 1882 Heinrich named Dörpfeld his assistant. Although he would not have accepted criticism or correction humbly a few years ago, the men of his staff had won his full respect. When they differed with him, he listened. By 1884 Heinrich had come to an unpleasant decision: he wanted to withdraw his book *Ilios* from print and rewrite it, for he was by now in reluctant agreement with Dörpfeld that not the third but the *second* city was sacred Troy.

He wrote, "My architects have proved to me that . . . I had not rightly distinguished and separated the two . . . settlements . . . the second and the third. . . . The Burnt City proper is, therefore, not the Third but the Second City."

It was a long way for him to come—to acknowledge his own error. Those close to him, Sophie and Dörpfeld, Virchow and Burnouf, knew how long a way it was. They understood that these admissions of error were costly, and his new-found humility endeared Heinrich to them. He was growing older. The years had brought him closer to the ideal of the true scholar and the disinterested searcher for truth. Not his personal prestige, but the provable truth was what mattered.

One day the staff members were relaxing at the close of work, having their glasses of ale and talking of Heinrich's amazing career. A younger man spoke about the Grave Circle at Mycenae.

"I wonder if we ever will know," he said, "whether the body you found, Dr. Schliemann, was Agamemnon's." There was an awkward silence. Dörpfeld cleared his throat. Not many years ago Heinrich would have given such a youngster a caustic reply. To his colleagues he seemed only very tired now, not in the least angry. When he did speak his tone was almost light.

"All right," he said slowly, and with surprising gentleness. "So we have found somebody named Schulze."

Nobody spoke of Agamemnon again. It was always "Schulze."

XX

"When the bright lamp of the sun had set, they went
to take their rest, each to his own house . . ."
Description of the gods. *Iliad*, I, 605-606

Agamemnon, king of men? Or "Schulze," identity unknown? Did it matter so very much, after all? The quarrels and the quibbles and the hairsplitting controversies
were beginning to exhaust him. He settled down in Athens,
in a home he designed for himself, where mementos of his
own past and mankind's would surround him and the family. He read his Homer. He gave classical names to his
servants and thanked the blessed gods for quiet, pleasant
days.

With Sophie and the two children Heinrich made a senti-
mental journey back to Ankershagen for a few months. It
was the homecoming of a man who could, if he wished,
wear decorations from royalty.

Minna was invited to visit them, and she came, a plump,
gray little matron, awed in the presence of one so famous.
How she had stirred his boy's heart he well remembered,
but it was a far distant memory, like that of the loss he had
felt when she married. He did his utmost to make her feel
at ease. And he turned the countryside upside down until
he located Hermann Niederhöffer, the student who had
recited lines of the *Iliad* in the grocery store. They read

Homer together, chuckling over that chance meeting which Heinrich had never forgotten. Carl Andres, who had taught him Latin lessons, often visited the family. He was now a recognized classical scholar and the curator of a museum in Neustrelitz.

Heinrich played games with his daughter, little Andromache, and young Agamemnon in the garden house near the lake called The Silver Chalice. He took their hands and led them to the haunted castle, wanting them to see and love all the places he had loved when he was a boy, among them the robber knight's grave in the village churchyard. The elderly sexton recognized his famous visitor.

"Ah, Mr. Schliemann," he said cordially, "as one familiar with our folklore and as an archeologist, you will be interested to hear of an unusual discovery we made here not long ago. When the church building was being repaired, workmen had to dig up the floor beneath the altar."

"Yes," said Heinrich, "and they found a man's leg bone!"

"That's quite right," the sexton remarked. "How did you guess?"

Agamemnon and his sister were wide-eyed, clinging to their father's hands.

"And it was the bone of the *right* leg?" By now Heinrich's eyes were sparkling merrily.

"It was," the mystified sexton agreed. "But I repeat: how did you guess?"

Heinrich replied solemnly, "I didn't guess," and the children took a firmer grasp of his fingers. "You see," he went on, "I once watched the *left* leg climb out of its grave!"

The sexton's smile was uncertain; he supposed that all great men must have their whimsical jokes.

And then it was time to leave Ankershagen. He had been idle long enough. Heinrich was restive and impatient to be putting spade to earth once more. There had been signal honors for him these last few months: he was made an honorary citizen of Berlin, a distinction granted only two others, Bismarck, and the great general, von Moltke. This was the sort of recognition that helped atone for some of the things his critics were saying about his labors at Troy.

With Dörpfeld in 1884 he now began excavating in Tiryns, a city almost as old and as glamorous with tradition as Mycenae. Heinrich took morning baths in the sea and spent his days in the sun and wind on the site. His workmen uncovered walls belonging to a palace. The same type of masonry had been found at Troy and wrongly identified as temple walls. Now that error could be corrected. They found potsherds and small objects here at Tiryns which resembled fragments taken out at Troy, and the coincidence forced Heinrich to make still further changes in his ideas about the discoveries at Hissarlik. It was always a wrench to his pride to say, "I was mistaken," but this was the penalty he must pay for the vast scope of his operations. He had pulled archeology out of the armchair and into the dust and wind of real places. His work was begun on a theoretical basis, but its tangible results obliged him to change and keep changing the theories themselves. What he found at Troy, for instance, threw light on what he unearthed at Mycenae and Tiryns. A dozen new questions sprang up for each one to which he supposed he had a definite and final answer.

As the digging at Hissarlik went on and on, one after

another of his theories fell apart under the impact of new findings. The "Scaean Gate" was just a very old gate; under it they were identifying even older gates. The "treasure of Priam" had been plucked from the remains of an ancient settlement, but in the layer of earth beneath that settlement they were now uncovering the ruins of a much grander palace.

He was disheartened and weary, and he missed Sophie. She could seldom join him these days, because the children and the household in Athens needed their full share of her attention. Heinrich had to content himself with infrequent visits and floods of letters from her. He turned often to his beloved *Iliad*, especially to the lines in Book XII which she knew by heart. Sophie would speak them to him when he was in a mood of discouragement as black as this one.

" '*O my friend*,' " she would quote, knowing that he would listen and respond with the serious, almost aloof smile only the two of them understood, " '*if escaping death in this fight would make us immortal forever, I would certainly not put myself in the front rank, nor would I let you take part in this struggle that brings men recognition. But since the evils of death, which no mortal can avoid or escape, await us anyway, let us go on, whether we bring fame to another or win it for ourselves.*' "

But she was not here on the hilltop with him to speak the words of reassurance. How he missed her! And there was no denying that Dörpfeld or Virchow or any of the others could carry on independently. He assured himself that Troy was bigger than any of them, himself included. Of course, he was being asked to address gatherings of internationally noted scientists, and this was some comfort. Two books were in the planning stage: one on Mycenae and one on Tiryns. For a while he drew apart from the physical labor and digging, because he simply had to rest. He went back to Athens again. This, too, was not like the old Heinrich. It was proof that he was getting on in years; he could not sustain the effort of a big campaign, much less direct it, as in past years.

But his self-exile from Troy was brief. Nothing could keep him at home and supposedly resting when he heard that he could get government permission to excavate on the site of Knossos, in Crete. He went there with Dörpfeld. They hired a crew. The owner of the hill where they wanted to dig was a shrewd bargainer. He held out for a price that seemed fantastic to Heinrich, who was willing to bargain up to a point; but when the man would not lower his price, Heinrich lost his temper, gave up, and departed. For one of the few times in his life the face of fortune was looking in the opposite direction. By leaving so impulsively Heinrich lost an opportunity to add the discovery of Crete's fabulous palace to his list of achievements. Nearly twenty years were to pass before the distinction of uncovering the splendor of Knossos would go to Sir Arthur Evans, the archeologist who worked the site from which Heinrich stalked away in anger.

Now he went to Cythera, an island in southern Ionia, where he excavated a temple to Aphrodite, one spoken of by Pausanias as well as Homer. It was enjoyable work, but it took a toll of Heinrich's strength as never before. He traveled to Egypt with Virchow in the winter of 1887 and again in 1888. The sea voyages helped him to recover from what he called his "nerves." But he was sixty-six, and he had driven himself without mercy.

Whenever he came back to Europe he returned to a chorus of criticism. A man named Ernst Bötticher, a former artillery captain, was firing the heaviest guns. He maintained that Heinrich's Trojan ruins were nothing more nor less than the remains of a cemetery. It was a war of words, and only that, but the attacks came from so many quarters that people who once hailed Heinrich as a genius were wondering whether he might in fact be a clever imposter.

Even his colleague Dörpfeld was urging him to retract some of the sweeping claims made in *Ilios*. The bronze key to a golden chest found in the Burnt City, said Dörpfeld (Dörpfeld his friend, his ally, his able and trusted helper!) was more probably a chisel. The "broken helmet"—well, perhaps a bowl. Some of the lance heads were surely the blades of knives. It came down to this: both scholars and lay people were arguing heatedly whether the Burnt City, or the second city, *or any city at all on Hissarlik* had been Homeric Troy. They argued with such flash and fire that he could not ignore them. His good name was at stake.

Heinrich decided to meet the loudest and most sarcastic of his critics on the site of the disputed ground. The German artillery captain was invited to roam around Hissarlik to his heart's content. He would be shown every courtesy: Heinrich insisted upon it. His pride had been stabbed to the quick. Two decades ago he probably would have challenged the captain to meet him and settle the affair with dueling rapiers. Now he felt only a heavy weight of discouragement.

When Bötticher finally arrived, Heinrich greeted him with icy politeness. "You are perfectly free, sir," he announced, "to go alone or with my staff members anywhere you wish on Hissarlik. My men are instructed to answer anything you may want to ask. You will prove for yourself that there has been no falsification, and that nothing we have found remotely resembles a cemetery."

The captain completed his survey a few days later. As the man was taking his leave, Heinrich was hopeful that he had relented and might retract some of his statements. They stood at the doorway of the stone house. "Until now I have not wished to interfere with your investigation," Heinrich said. "But of course all your questions have been answered. I am confident that by this time you agree that our findings are, historically, of the utmost significance."

"You are mistaken," said Bötticher stiffly. "I have seen nothing, nothing at all, that alters my original contention by one iota. Good day, *Doctor* Schliemann!"

Tears came to the old man's eyes as he watched the captain march away. He leaned for a moment against the door, anguished. Was he to be mocked for his life's work?

Other blows fell. Several museums declined his offers of collections from Troy and Mycenae. Nothing hurt quite so badly; this was the most cutting criticism of all.

During the following year a conference was held at Troy. Scholars came by invitation from England, Germany, Turkey, America—a dozen nations. These men went thoroughly over the site. Later they published their conclusions: in their opinion, not the third, or Burnt City, but the second settlement, was Troy of the *Iliad*.

And most of these days Heinrich was in pain with an

infection of the ear that interfered with his work and his sleep at night. He went to Germany in November of 1890 to undergo surgery, but the pain was only slightly relieved. Doctors warned against his traveling or exerting himself too soon after the operation. He missed Sophie grievously. Her letters telling about the children and the antics of their pet dog and the family cats and ducks made him homesick. He was a German in his heart of hearts, and Christmas was coming. He longed to be home to light candles on the tree and smell the delectable fragrance of roasting goose. Citizen of the United States he might be, Russia he loved as his second motherland, and in things of the spirit he often felt himself to be Greek; but all else apart, he was a German, and it was almost Christmastime.

Before leaving for his home in Athens he had business matters to take up with his publisher, at Leipzig, and naturally he must see Virchow in Berlin. They optimistically talked over plans for another trip together and for next year's campaign at Hissarlik, where Dörpfeld would again join them. They discussed a new and better arrangement for the display of the Schliemann collection—his Trojan treasures—in the Berlin People's Museum.

Although he was still in pain and looking worn, Heinrich could not resist making a side trip to Naples. He spent two days here studying the newest acquisitions of antique objects in the museum. And when he heard that there had been fresh excavations at Pompeii, cold as the weather was, and ill as he felt, he had to go and see the results.

Sophie and the children expected him for Christmas. But the pain grew suddenly very severe and he wired Sophie that he would be delayed. This was his last message. On the twenty-sixth of December Sophie was notified by the doctors who were attending him that Heinrich had collapsed and had been found dying on a street in Naples. The infection had spread rapidly to both ears and attacked the brain. Before she could possibly reach the hospital where he had been taken—even before she could leave Athens—she had a second message: he was dead.

The body was escorted to Athens by his beloved colleague, Wilhelm Dörpfeld.

At the final services King George and the Crown Prince of Greece were present. Men of letters and science and art were in the throng that came to hear Heinrich honored for the last time. A. Loudon Snowden, American Minister to Greece, paid tribute to him for having been a citizen of America as well as Germany. Snowden's words were spoken with feeling, because archeology was one of his own enthusiasms; he was a sponsor of the new American school of archeology in Athens. Messages of sympathy came from all parts of the world.

The final speaker was Dörpfeld. "Rest in peace," he said softly to his colleague. "You have done enough."

At the head of the casket throughout the service stood a bust of Homer, whose words Heinrich Schliemann loved beyond all others, and whose poems inspired his major work. He had restored Troy to her place in the sun, and he had redeemed from darkness buried cities of the Age of Heroes on the Greek mainland. It was indeed time to rest.

His body was laid in the soil of Greece, not too distant from the wine-dark sea.

EPILOGUE

Heinrich Schliemann died knowing that he could not rightly lay claim to finding the Troy of Homer and Priam. About the great treasure of Troy and the golden masks of Mycenae there were many questions. The puzzles he left unsolved were more complicated than the one he had thought to solve for all time. What, then, had he achieved?

After Schliemann's death Dörpfeld went on studying at Troy for three years. He uncovered sections of walls and buildings of a city far larger than the Burnt, or second, City. Dörpfeld thought this the most important of any that had been on the hill of Hissarlik, and he called it Troy VI. His excavations proved it to be much larger in area and significance than Schliemann had estimated.

For some thirty years after Dörpfeld stopped working there, the hill lay silent and deserted. The attention of archeologists was being drawn elsewhere in the Aegean area. Schliemann's work at Troy and at Mycenae and Tiryns had brought about a surge of interest in prehistoric sites. Now came years of discoveries so brilliant that for a time Troy was almost forgotten. Sir Arthur Evans at Knossos, in Crete, found and reconstructed the fabled Palace of Minos. In the Aegean islands many Bronze Age sites were explored, and with exciting results. On the Greek mainland, in particular at Mycenae, British archeologists under the direction of Prof. A. J. B. Wace made new excavations in the 1920's at places where Schliemann had dug first. Greek archeologists followed after the British at Mycenae, so that today a second royal Grave Circle has been uncovered on the acropolis, and other tombs as well. The area of the Aegean was being systematically excavated. Our interpretation of history has been drastically altered by the findings.

During the early 1930's Troy again came to the forefront. Because so much prehistoric material was being discovered all over the mainland of Greece and in the Aegean islands, it was deemed wise to go back and restudy Troy. Under the leadership of the distinguished archeologist Dr. Carl Blegen, an expedition of Americans from the University of Cincinnati returned to probe the mound of Hissarlik once more. From 1932 to 1938 they went painstakingly over the ground Schliemann first dug in 1870.

So we see that archeologists of many nations have been intently studying the Aegean area in the years after Schliemann's death. In a very real sense Schliemann is responsible for this leap in archeological and historical discovery. Our ever-growing fund of knowledge about the Bronze Age civilizations is due to him. He stood at the door and pointed the way. This is one of the signal achievements of the pastor's son.

Troy came to be Schliemann's very life. He invested years of effort in its excavation. Perhaps we should consider briefly what modern study has revealed about it.

What *is* Troy?

The nine cities that have occupied the hill of Hissarlik extend back in time more than five thousand years. Each one, we now know, was walled, and each grew to be larger than the city it succeeded. The later cities literally spilled over the side of the hill and onto the Plain of Troy. Within each of these nine, many different building "phases," as the archeologist calls them, can be determined. Only recently have the "phases" been thoroughly disentangled. Probably the term "periods" is the clearest one to use, rather than "phases." It serves as a reminder that within the time a city—any city, ancient or modern—flourishes, there will be buildings of several different periods and styles of architecture contained within it. So it was with the cities of Troy.

The nine are formally designated as Troy I to Troy IX. Dr. Carl Blegen found Troy I to be of imposing proportions, and he placed it at the beginning of the Bronze Age. When we refer to Troy II, the Burnt City, we are speaking of the second city counting upward from the bottom. Although Dörpfeld considered Troy VI to be Homeric Troy, excavators now believe that what they call Troy VII-A was the city of Homer's poems, because Troy VI seems to have been destroyed by an earthquake and was soon rebuilt by the survivors, who put up new buildings on the rubble of the old. Troy VIII belongs to the Hellenistic era, and Troy IX to the Roman, as Schliemann himself well knew.

One can best appreciate the enormity of the interpreter's task, looking at the cut-away layers of earth on Hissarlik, if one understands, then, that Troy I is a deposit containing traces of a city with no fewer than *ten* prehistoric building periods. Troy VI includes *eight* building periods of Bronze Age times, and Troy IX has *three* building periods of late

Roman times. The grand total comes to forty-six. Forty-six building periods within the nine cities of Troy!

Small wonder that Schliemann made errors in interpreting what he found!

Knowing as we do today that Troy VII-A is the Homeric city, we know also that the jewels Sophie Schliemann scooped out with her fingers were never worn by Helen of Troy; these came instead from Troy II, laid waste a thousand years earlier. At first Schliemann could not bear to think that Homer had never laid eyes on the Burnt City. But today's field workers can state that the Burnt City represents a town that had disappeared into the misty past at the time when Homer wrote; and we think that he lived some seven or eight hundred years before Jesus. If Homer had visited the Plain of Troy sometime in the ninth century, he would have seen no city at all on the hill of Hissarlik. Everything on it had been covered up and the hilltop was overgrown. The Trojan War had been fought centuries before Homer lived. Taking the traditional date of 1180 B.C. as the year of Troy's capture, we see that its site would have been unoccupied in Homer's lifetime. No city was to be built on it again until the Hellenistic Age.

The memories of a long war and a powerful city had endured. Traditions about both of them were a part of Homer's heritage. When he composed his poems, he re-created in them the old tales of his land, brightening and livening them with the genius of his imagination. It was hardly necessary for Homer to have seen Troy, as Schliemann at first supposed.

We know now that the golden masks of Mycenae did

not cover the faces of Agamemnon and his captains. Still, archeologists quite generally agree that there could have been such a person as Agamemnon in preclassical times, and no one laughs at Schliemann for assuming that he found the warrior's tomb. The all-important fact is that his discoveries were epoch-making. Out of his hunches and guesswork came mistakes. They were not small mistakes. Excavators would give much to be able to examine the classical-period buildings he tore apart in his eagerness to get to "Troy." To gain access to unexplored sections of Hissarlik today they must move tons of earth, his early dump heaps, which stand in their way. Schliemann did leave a number of "islands" or columns of unexplored earth, and their recent study has been fruitful.

How might we finally sum up the lasting achievements of Heinrich Schliemann? We have noted that the great renewal of interest in excavation and research is part of our debt to him; there are other reasons why we owe him recognition.

He never realized the full extent of the proud cultures whose traces he had revealed at Troy, Mycenae, and Tiryns. Before him, no one even guessed that these cultures had existed in the Aegean world. This fact is of greater moment for our understanding of the currents of Western civilization than if Schliemann had been correct in his wistful belief that he had cleared the dirt from the actual flagstoned streets of Homer's Troy. Before he died, this belief of his was sharply challenged. In the final tired years he admitted that he simply could not be sure. What he did achieve was of larger import: he enabled us to push past the boundaries of the Heroic Age and to catch glimpses of its grandeur. We have learned infinitely more about the people of that long-ago era. This one achievement is of tremendous significance. It is far more important than Schliemann lived to know.

Pausanias and Homer were the guides Schliemann followed. Fascinating and very touching is the fact that his faith in their accuracy led him to every one of his boldest discoveries, although he was not correct in what he thought he had found, at either Troy or Mycenae. He set out to locate only one Troy. As early as 1871, while the work on Hissarlik was barely begun, he wrote:

"My expectations are extremely modest; I have no hope of finding plastic works of art. The single object of my excavations from the beginning was only to find Troy, whose site has been discussed by a hundred scholars in a hundred books, but which as yet no one has ever sought to bring to life by excavation."

Schliemann never quite understood that when Pausanias retold the tales of war and scandal that were old in his day, and when he described monuments and cities in his guidebook, he was often repeating legends combined with myths that had been handed down to him as was the story of the Trojan War to Homer. The marvel is that in directing himself by these descriptions, Schliemann found such riches. He flung open for us the gates into a Bronze Age past where commoners and nobles loved life fiercely and lived it fully, as we can see from the work of their craftsmen, the daring designs of their experimenting architects, and in the humblest and starkly beautiful clay vessels made for an ordinary man's oil or wine.

Certainly he made errors. Yes, he destroyed some ruins.

A field worker today has precision instruments because their need was demonstrated and they were devised. Schliemann had to improvise a number of techniques. He was, for instance, the first archeologist to see how important pottery fragments are as a means of establishing historical periods. Little can bring such an appreciative glint to the archeologist's eye as the discovery of an undisturbed ancient rubbish heap. The story of prehistoric man is often ably interpreted through his trash piles. Early man was always too busy keeping his children fed, his day's work done, his roof repaired, and his wall mended to trouble his head about written records. Record-keeping he left to the scribes and priests. Ancient man just lived. His streets gathered rubbish from his wife's broom. When the litter outside the door piled too high, it was shoveled out of the streets into an alley or over the side of a convenient cliff. If warfare or earthquake leveled his house and by the grace of the gods he survived, he spat on his hands and built himself a new one, usually without waiting to mop up all the ruins of the old. He pitched his oyster shells out the door, and sometimes he buried his dead under the bedroom floor until the crowded conditions of town life imposed more orderly ways upon him. That is what civilization— the living together of people in cities—invariably demands.

By studying the same types of potsherds as those preserved by Schliemann, archeologists have worked out tentative historical periods as clues to the age of the ruins they are investigating. To the objective field worker, a broken clay pot can tell a dramatic tale. Where it lies in the subsoil of earth and rubbish; whether or not it was made on a potter's wheel; from what sort of clay it was cast, and how shaped, painted, glazed, and fired—all these are vital clues to the cultural development of the people who used it. As the plundered tombs of the Pharaohs testify, gold and jewels are not likely to stay safe in their most secret hiding places, because they are lures for thieves. But a chip of clay pot usually remains undisturbed where it lies once it is tossed away. It is a tribute to the wisdom of Schliemann that he recognized the value of studying potsherds.

In the final reckoning, it matters not very much to us that Schliemann was wrong in thinking he had found Homeric Troy. It does matter that he brought up evidences of a civilization centuries older than the legends wreathed about Troy. We owe to him our certainty that the hill of Hissarlik was a citadel for centuries, vigorous and unrivaled in its control of the Troad and the Dardanelles. We comprehend old wars better by realizing that economic rivalry lay behind the Greek and Trojan quarrel in which their most potent gods took sides. The Argives had more than Helen to gain by conquering sacred Troy. The Troad, the Dardanelles, and immensely profitable trade routes were their prizes: mastery of the Aegean world. Because the jade ax Schliemann found at Troy must have come from China, and because flint of the sort he unearthed was quarried nowhere in the Troad but had been imported, perhaps from Egypt, we can infer that the old trade routes were far-flung and efficient. Thus we know more about our ancestors than that they were vain and quarrelsome and loved to decorate themselves with gold ornaments.

We know, too, from the bones of animals dug out of Hissarlik that Homer's description of the Trojans as the "horse-taming Trojans" was historically correct. The Cincinnati Expedition workers have shown that the horse first reached Troy in an early period of the sixth city. We can see for ourselves what animals were domesticated, which ones were used for food, and which were ritually sacrificed to the gods. From splinters of charred bone, potsherds, and toppled building stones we can reconstruct a vanished people's way of life.

Before Schliemann presented the evidence, confused and complex as it was, on which to build new interpretations, we had no systematic knowledge of Aegean history. We did not know that there had been *any* Troy. We owe him this.

Before he went to work with his raging energy and winged imagination, we could only guess about the way man had lived in Greece and Asia Minor in the years before the classical periods of history. He was not alive to see what younger men and women would discover when they followed in his footsteps across the Troad and the mainland of Greece. When they studied the ruins he had located, then made new findings in the earth where he first ventured, his work combined with theirs made it possible to begin piecing together the details of the whole stirring story.

As an old man Schliemann saw many of his dearest beliefs held up to ridicule. He had to learn that scholarship demands the discipline of humility. He sorrowed that his work at Troy raised more questions than it answered. He went too fast and he destroyed some evidence that it would be useful to have. He rushed into print with theories that could not be proved.

But none of these very human tendencies lessens the value of his lasting contributions. "The year 1870 really stands at a turning point in the archaeological highway," said Carl Blegen in 1940, just seventy years after Schliemann began excavating Troy. ". . . With Schliemann came our first considerable knowledge of the preclassical world in Greek lands; furthermore, with Schliemann, one may fairly maintain, a new spirit entered into archaeological research and modern field archaeology was conceived."

Will Durant reminds us that Schliemann's experience should warn us to be skeptical even of our skepticism. "There never was a Troy," said the complacent scholars of Schliemann's youth. He proved them wrong. "You couldn't find it even if it did exist," said other authorities. He found not one, but nine Troys in all. "You're an amateur, uneducated and untrained; you have no right to invade our territory." But he was a man possessed by an idea, and in carrying it out he unrolled new vistas of human life.

Once when he was feeling most tired, the arguments about what he had or had not found seemed to hover around him like gadflies. His labors seemed thankless. Still, he was philosophical. He said thoughtfully, "The truth will emerge and be accepted—although perhaps it will be only after my death."

Without his stubborn and passionate faith, and without his iron determination, we could be wondering to this day about the buried city of Troy and the life of Bronze Age people. Our debt to him is almost beyond measuring.

TIME CHART

	Egypt	Greece	Troy	B.C.*
NEW STONE AGE		Of uncertain duration		to about 4000
COPPER AGE		A period of transition		
BRONZE AGE				3500-1200
Early	Old Kingdom		Cities I-V	3000-2000
Middle	Middle Kingdom	Crete at its height, 1600-1400	Cities VI-VII	2000-1600
Late	New Kingdom	Mycenae and	City VII-A	1600-1200
		Tiryns powerful		
		Trojan War		1180
IRON AGE				1100-900
HELLENIC AGE				900-338
Heroic Age—Age of Kings and Heroes				
Homer: *The Iliad, The Odyssey*				800?
Age of Tyrants			Troy VIII?	700-500
Pisistratus of Athens				
Polycrates of Samos				
Age of Democracy				500-429
Reforms of Cleisthenes				

Start of the Persian Wars
  Battle of Marathon, 490
Pericles and "the Golden Days"—mid-Fifth Century
  Herodotus
  Phidias
  Hippocrates
  Aeschylus, Sophocles, Euripides, Aristophanes
Decline of Hellenic Culture . . . . 431 onward
  Peloponnesian War begins, 431
  Plato

HELLENISTIC AGE . . . . *Troy IX*   338-146
  Alexander conquers the Near East and Persia   336-323
  Euclid
  Eratosthenes
  Archimedes

ROMAN CONQUEST OF GREECE 146
  Strabo, 63 B.C.–24 A.D.
  Pausanias, Second Century A.D.   A.D.

* Some dates, especially those before 500 B.C., are tentative.

Adapted from *Civilization Past and Present*, Vol. I, by Wallbank and Taylor. Copyright 1942 by Scott, Foresman and Company, Chicago. Used by permission.

BIBLIOGRAPHY

Blegen, Carl W., Caskey, John L., Rawson, Marion, and Sperling, Jerome. *Troy*, Volumes I, II, III, IV. Princeton, N. J.: Princeton University Press for the University of Cincinnati, 1950, 1951, 1953, 1958.

Durant, Will. *The Life of Greece*. New York: Simon and Schuster, 1939.

Homer. *The Iliad*. Loeb Classical Library. Cambridge, Mass.: Harvard University Press, 1946.

———. *The Odyssey*. Loeb Classical Library. Cambridge, Mass.: Harvard University Press, 1946.

Lorimer, H. L. *Homer and the Monuments*. London: Macmillan and Company, Ltd., 1950.

Ludwig, Emil. *Schliemann, The Story of a Gold-Seeker*. Boston: Little, Brown and Company, 1931.

Pausanias. *Description of Greece*. Loeb Classical Library. New York: G. P. Putnam's Sons, 1931.

Schliemann, Heinrich. *Ilios*. New York: Harper and Brothers, 1880.

———. *Mycenae*. London: John Murray, 1878.

———. *Tiryns*. London: John Murray, 1886.

———. *Troja*. London: John Murray, 1884.

Schliemann, Sophie, ed. *Heinrich Schliemann's Selbstbiographie*. Leipzig: F. A. Brockhaus, 1892.

Schuchhardt, C. *Schliemann's Excavations*. London and New York: Macmillan and Company, Ltd., 1891.

Tsountas, Chrestos, and Manatt, J. Irving. *The Mycenaean Age*. Boston and New York: Houghton, Mifflin Company, 1897.

Virgil. *The Aeneid*. Loeb Classical Library. Cambridge, Mass.: Harvard University Press, 1947.

Wace, Alan J. B. *Mycenae, an Archeological History and Guide*. Princeton, N. J.: Princeton University Press, 1949.

Weber, Shirley H., ed. *Schliemann's First Visit to America, 1850-1851*. Cambridge, Mass.: Harvard University Press for the American School of Classical Studies in Athens, 1942.

INDEX

VOYAGER BOOKS

Karin Anckarsvärd
**THE MYSTERIOUS
SCHOOLMASTER**

Nina Brown Baker
NICKELS AND DIMES

George Barrow
**YOUR WORLD
IN MOTION**

Margot Benary-Isbert
BLUE MYSTERY

L. M. Boston
**THE RIVER AT
GREEN KNOWE**

Marjorie Braymer
**THE WALLS OF
WINDY TROY**

Roger Burlingame
**INVENTORS BEHIND
THE INVENTOR**

Madye Lee Chastain
**EMMY KEEPS
A PROMISE**

Elizabeth K. Cooper
**SCIENCE IN YOUR
OWN BACK YARD**

Helen F. Daringer
STEPSISTER SALLY

Edward Eager
KNIGHT'S CASTLE

Elizabeth Enright
GONE-AWAY LAKE

Eleanor Estes
THE WITCH FAMILY

C. H. Frick
THE COMEBACK GUY

László Hámori
**DANGEROUS
JOURNEY**

Mary C. Hatch
13 DANISH TALES

Carolyn Haywood
HERE'S A PENNY

Ivan Kušan
**THE MYSTERY
OF GREEN HILL**

Mildred Lawrence
PEACHTREE ISLAND

Dorothy Lyons
DARK SUNSHINE

C. J. Maginley
**HISTORIC MODELS
OF EARLY AMERICA**

Stephen W. Meader
BULLDOZER

Mary Norton
THE BORROWERS

Helen Rushmore
**COWBOY JOE OF
THE CIRCLE S**

Carl Sandburg
WIND SONG

Leo Schneider
**YOU AND YOUR
SENSES**

Virginia Sorensen
PLAIN GIRL

E. C. Spykman
**TERRIBLE,
HORRIBLE EDIE**

William O. Steele
THE PERILOUS ROAD

Alfred Stefferud
**THE WONDERS
OF SEEDS**

Yoshiko Uchida
**THE MAGIC
LISTENING CAP**

Henry Winterfeld
**DETECTIVES IN
TOGAS**